PLATO'S MENO

The Focus Philosophical Library

PLATO'S MENO

Translation and Annotations

George Anastaplo
Laurence Berns

Focus Publishing
R. Pullins Co.
Newburyport, MA
www.pullins.com

Plato
Meno
© 2004 George Anastaplo and Laurence Berns

Focus Publishing/R. Pullins Company
PO Box 369
Newburyport MA 01950
www.pullins.com

Cover: Torpedo Fish (in sections 80A-B, Meno, when asked by Socrates to define virtue, compares Socrates to the torpedo fish, which stuns its victims into perplexity.)

ISBN: 978-0-941051-71-2

To see available eBook versions, visit www.pullins.com

Printed in the United States of America

15 14 13 12 11 10 9 8 7 6

0713TS

CONTENTS

To

John Gormly

(1925-1967)

fellow student at the University of Chicago

INTRODUCTION

The *Meno* has traditionally served as an introduction to Plato's two dozen dialogues, if not also to the millennia-long philosophic enterprise itself. Elementary questions are raised in this dialogue not only about virtue and how it may be acquired, but also about inquiry and its proper objects, about knowledge and its relation to opinion, and about the connections between learning and teaching. The dramatic form of a dialogue suggests that the character, circumstances, and actions of its participants, along with their speeches, are to be taken into account by the reader.

We attempt to provide here, with a minimum of intrusion by us in the dialogue text itself, a reliable sense of what Plato has his four characters (Socrates, Meno, the Slave-boy, and Anytus) say and do. An attempt has been made, for example, to be as consistent in our translation of Greek terms as is in accordance with familiar English usage. Departures from such consistency are recorded in the endnotes. Whenever Socrates seems to deviate from what would be ordinary usage in any language, we translate literally, on the assumption that we are intended to think about what these deviations mean. Also recorded in the endnotes is other information that it may help the reader eventually to have.

In addition to the traditional Stephanus page numbers for the dialogue (set forth in the outer margins of the text), we have provided numbers for the Speeches. This innovation should be useful both for beginning students and for classroom discussions, without interfering with the work of more advanced students. The illustrations for the steps taken by Socrates and the Slave-boy in their celebrated geometrical explorations are presented in unprecedented detail (in Appendix B of this volume). Such detail can help counteract the habit of the modern student of mathematics to leap as quickly as possible to the solution of a problem. We assume, that is, that Socrates is trying to reveal in detail all the steps that may be presupposed by such a mathematical problem: that is, he is interested in how one comes to understand the problem and its solution, and hence what the principles are through which it is understood.

The endnotes annotating the text of the dialogue are keyed to our new Speech numbers, along with the old Stephanus numbers, but without reference to those notes in the text itself to distract the reader of the dialogue. Many readers, once it is understood who is talking and perhaps where and when, should be able to go through this dialogue without consulting any notes, except perhaps for the geometrical illustrations provided in the note for Speech 356 (86E-87B) and Appendix B of this volume. (Thus, an attempt has been made by us to permit the reader of English to come to our text much as the reader of Greek might come to Plato's original text.) Some of the endnotes provide elementary information about now-obscure references in the text, other of them are about implications of Greek words and wordplay that no translation can convey; still others are designed to help the reader address some of the more difficult questions raised by the dialogue. The endnotes also include references to other Platonic dialogues and to some ancient and modern texts where various questions touched upon in the *Meno* are treated in much greater detail than it is useful to do here. (More than one-fourth of the Speeches in the *Meno* have at least one endnote provided for them in this volume.)

Most of the exchanges in the dialogue are between Socrates, an Athenian, and Meno, a Thessalian visiting Athens. The time of the dialogue seems to be not long before Meno leaves Greece for an ill-fated military expedition in Persia. (It is well to keep in mind that the privileged Meno, for all his limitations, does seem to be able to follow easily the geometrical exercises that Socrates uses.) The infamous capital prosecution of Socrates (in 399 BCE) evidently occurred shortly after his supposed conversation presented here with Anytus, a local politician who turned out to be one of Socrates' three accusers. It is not certain precisely where in Athens this dialogue takes place or how many are present to witness its exchanges.

We have consulted, from the beginning of our joint effort, the translation of the *Meno* prepared in the 1960s by John Gormly for the Basic Program of Liberal Education for Adults at the University of Chicago. This is the Program in which both of us began our teaching careers half a century ago.

In the main, we have used for the Greek text the Oxford edition of John Burnet. Other Greek texts drawn upon by us are indicated in the endnotes, along with references to those few occasions when we have departed from the standard modern versions of the Greek text. We have also made considerable use of the grammatical and interpretive notes in the Greek text of *Meno* in the Alfred Mollin and Robert Williamson volume, *An Introduction to Ancient Greek.*

George Anastaplo
CHICAGO, ILLINOIS

Laurence Berns
ANNAPOLIS, MARYLAND

PLATO'S *MENO*

[Or, About Virtue: Testing]

The Characters of the Dialogue:
   MENO   SOCRATES   MENO'S [SLAVE] BOY   ANYTUS

[1]   MENO: Can you tell me, Socrates, whether virtue is   70A
something teachable? Or is it not teachable, but something
that comes from practice? Or is it something neither from
practice nor from learning, but something that comes to
human beings by nature, or some other way?

[2]   SOCRATES: Meno, it used to be that Thessalians were well-
reputed among the Greeks and were admired both for
horsemanship and for wealth, but now, it seems to me,
they are to be admired for wisdom also; and not least of   70B
them the fellow citizens of your comrade, Aristippus, the
Larissians. And the one responsible for this happening
to you is Gorgias. For when he came to the city, he
captivated the foremost men among the Aleudai as lovers
of wisdom, of whom your lover Aristippus is one, and the
foremost of the other Thessalians too. And in particular
this is the habit to which he has habituated you, namely,
of answering both fearlessly and magnificently whenever
anyone asks you anything, as is fitting for those who
know; inasmuch, indeed, as he makes himself available   70C
to any Greek who wants to question him about whatever
one might wish to ask, and there is no one whom he does
not answer. But hereabouts, dear Meno, the opposite   71A
condition prevails: it's as if some sort of drought of
wisdom has come about, and there seems to be a danger
that wisdom has left these parts for yours. And so, if you

1

are willing to ask anyone hereabouts such a question, there is no one who will not laugh and say, "Stranger, I seem to be in danger of your thinking me to be someone who is blessed—to know about virtue, whether it is something teachable or in what way it comes about. But I am so far from knowing about virtue, whether it is something teachable or not teachable, that I happen not to know at all what that thing virtue itself is."

71B   And I myself, Meno, am in this condition, too. I share the poverty of my fellow citizens in this matter and blame myself for not knowing about virtue at all. And how could I know what sort of thing something is, if I do not know what it is? Or does it seem possible to you that someone who has no cognizance of Meno at all, who he is, could know whether he is handsome or rich or well-born, or the opposite of these? Does it seem possible to you?

71C   [3]   MENO: Not to me. But do you, Socrates, truly not know what virtue is, and is this really what we should report about you back home?

[4]   SOCRATES: Not only that, comrade, but also that I never yet happened to meet anyone else who, in my opinion, did know.

[5]   MENO: What? You didn't happen to meet Gorgias when he was here?

[6]   SOCRATES: I did.

[7]   MENO: Really– did he not seem to you to know?

[8]   SOCRATES: I'm not a very good rememberer, Meno, so I'm not able to say at present how he seemed to me then. But, perhaps, he did know, and you know what he used to say.

71D   Then, remind me how he said it. Or, if you wish, speak yourself, for you, surely, share his opinion.

[9]   MENO: I do.

[10]   SOCRATES: Then let's let him go, since, in fact, he is not here. But you yourself, by the gods, Meno, what do you declare virtue to be? Speak and don't be begrudging, so that I will have fabricated a most fortunate falsehood if it becomes evident that you and Gorgias do know, while I've stated that I never happened to come across anyone who knew.

71E   [11]   MENO: But it's not hard to tell, Socrates. First, then, if it's the virtue of a man you want, it's easy to say that this is the virtue of a man: to be sufficient to carry on the affairs of the city and while carrying them on to do well by his friends and harm to his enemies and to take care that he not suffer any such thing himself. And if it's the virtue of a woman you want, that's not hard to go through, in that she needs to manage the household well, conserving what is inside and being obedient to her man. And the virtue of a child is different, both female and male, and of an elderly man, and, if you want, of a freeman or, if you 72A want, of a slave. And there are a great many other virtues, so that there is no difficulty in speaking about what virtue is. For according to each activity and each time of life relative to each task for each of us there is a virtue, and in the same way, I suppose, Socrates, there is also a vice.

[12]   SOCRATES: I seem to have hit upon some great good fortune, Meno, if, while seeking one virtue I have discovered a sort of swarm of virtues gathered about you. But, Meno, following up this image about swarms, if after you had been asked by me about the very being of a bee, 72B just what it is, and you were saying that there are many and of all sorts, what would you answer me if I asked you: "Then are you saying that they are many and of all sorts and different from one another in this by which they are bees? Or that it is not this in which they differ, but in something else, such as beauty or size or something else of this sort?" Tell me, what would you answer after being questioned in this way?

[13]   MENO: I would answer this, that they do not differ, one from the other, in that by which they are bees.

[14]   SOCRATES: If then I were to say after that: "Tell me further, 72C Meno, this very thing in which they do not differ but are all the same thing, what do you say that is?" You could, I suppose, tell me what it is?

[15]   MENO: I could.

[16]   SOCRATES: And so too, surely, about the virtues: even if they are many and of all sorts, still they all have some one and the same form through which they are virtues and upon which one would somehow do well to focus one's gaze, that is, the one answering him who has asked him to clarify that, namely, what does virtue happen to be. Or 72D do you not understand what I'm saying?

[17]   MENO: It seems to me that I do understand. Yet somehow I don't grasp what is being asked as well as I would like.

[18]   SOCRATES: Is it about virtue only that you think in this way, Meno, that there is one for a man and another for a woman and the others; or do you think the same way about health and about size and about strength? Does the health of a man seem to you to be one thing and the health of a woman another? Or is it the same form everywhere, if it is indeed health, whether it exists in a man or in anyone else whatever?

72E

[19]   MENO: Health, at any rate, does seem to me to be the same both for a man and for a woman.

[20]   SOCRATES: And not then also size and strength? If a woman is really strong, will she not be strong by the same form and by the same strength? For "by the same" I mean this: strength does not differ with respect to being strength whether it exists in a man or in a woman. Or does it seem to you that there is some difference?

[21]   MENO: Not to me.

73A

[22]   SOCRATES: And will virtue differ in some way, with respect to its being virtue, whether it exists in a child or in an old man or in a woman or in a man?

[23]   MENO: It somehow seems to me, at any rate, Socrates, that this is no longer like those others.

[24]   SOCRATES: But why? Were you not saying that the virtue of a man is to manage a city well, and that of a woman, a household?

[25]   MENO: I was.

[26]   SOCRATES: Then can one manage a city well, or a household, or anything else whatever, if one does not manage it moderately and justly?

[27]   MENO: Surely not.

73B

[28]   SOCRATES: Then if people really manage justly and moderately, will they manage by justice and moderation?

[29]   MENO: Necessarily.

[30]   SOCRATES: Then both need the same things, if they really intend to be good, both the woman and the man, namely,

justice and moderation.

[31] MENO: So it appears.

[32] SOCRATES: What about a child and an old man? If they should be licentious and unjust, could they ever become good?

[33] MENO: Surely not.

[34] SOCRATES: But if they are moderate and just?

[35] MENO: Yes.

[36] SOCRATES: Then all human beings are good in the same 73C way; for it is from the same things that they happen to become good.

[37] MENO: It seems likely.

[38] SOCRATES: They would surely not be good in the same way if they didn't have the same virtue.

[39] MENO: Surely not.

[40] SOCRATES: Since, therefore, virtue is the same for all, try to say and to recollect what that very thing is which Gorgias, and you with him, affirm it to be.

[41] MENO: What else than to be able to rule over human beings—if indeed you are seeking some one thing concerning all of them?

[42] SOCRATES: But certainly I do seek that. But then, is the 73D virtue of both a child, Meno, and a slave the same, for the two of them to be able to rule the master, and does it seem to you that he who rules would still be a slave?

[43] MENO: It does not at all seem so to me, Socrates.

[44] SOCRATES: Since, my very good man, it is not likely. Then also observe the following: "to be able to rule," you say. Shall we not add to that "justly, but not unjustly"?

[45] MENO: I, at any rate, think so. For justice, Socrates, is virtue.

[46] SOCRATES: Is it virtue, Meno, or some particular virtue? 73E

[47] MENO: How do you mean that?

[48] SOCRATES: Just as about anything else whatever. For example, about roundness, if you want, I would say that it is a particular shape, not just simply that it is shape.

The reason I would speak in this way is that there are also other shapes.

[49]   MENO: What you say is quite right, for I too say that there is not only justice, but that there are also other virtues.

74A   [50]   SOCRATES: What are these? Tell me. Just as I too could tell you that there are also other shapes, if you were to order me to do so, you too then tell me other virtues.

[51]   MENO: Well then, courage seems to me, at any rate, to be a virtue, and moderation, and wisdom, and magnificence, and a great many others.

[52]   SOCRATES: Again, Meno, we have suffered the same thing. Although seeking one, we have found many virtues, but in another way than we did just now. But the one which exists throughout all of these we are not able to find out.

[53]   MENO: No, for I am somehow not able to grasp, Socrates, as you seek it, one virtue from all, as I can in the other cases.

74B

[54]   SOCRATES: That is likely. But I am quite willing, if I am able, to help us advance. For you understand, I suppose, that this is how it holds for everything. If someone were to ask you this, which I was just now speaking of, "What is shape, Meno?"—and if you were to say to him that it is roundness, and if he were to say to you what I did, "Is roundness shape, or a particular shape?", you would surely say that it is a particular shape.

[55]   MENO: Certainly, I would.

74C   [56]   SOCRATES: Is it not because of this, that there are also other shapes?

[57]   MENO: Yes.

[58]   SOCRATES: And if he were to ask you further what sorts of shapes, you would tell him?

[59]   MENO: I would.

[60]   SOCRATES: And again, if he were to ask you about color in the same way, what it is, and you said that it is white, and after that the questioner took it up, asking, "Is the white color a particular color?", you would say that it is a particular color because there also happen to be other colors?

[61]   MENO: I would.

[62]   SOCRATES: And if then he ordered you to tell other colors, would you speak of others that happen to be colors no less than white is?   74D

[63]   MENO: Yes.

[64]   SOCRATES: If then he, just as I, was following up the argument and said, "We always arrive at many, but this is not what I'm seeking. But since you address these many by some one name and you say of none of them that they are not shape, even those that are opposite to one another, what is this that comprises the round or the straight, which indeed you name shape, and you affirm that the   74E round is no more shape than the straight?" Or is this not the way that you speak?

[65]   MENO: I do.

[66]   SOCRATES: Whenever you do speak in this way, do you then affirm that the round is no more round than straight and that the straight is no more straight than round?

[67]   MENO: Certainly not, Socrates.

[68]   SOCRATES: But, indeed, you do affirm that the round is no more a shape than the straight, the one no more than the other.

[69]   MENO: You speak the truth.

[70]   SOCRATES: Whatever then is this of which this is the name: shape? Try to say. If then you had said to someone   75A questioning in this way either about shape or about color, "But I don't understand what you want, fellow, nor do I know what you mean," probably he would have wondered and said, "You do not understand that what I am seeking is that which is the same over all of these?" Or would you not be able to tell about these things, Meno, if someone had asked you: "What is it that is over the round and the straight and the others, and is the same over all of those things which you, indeed, call shapes?" Try to say it, so that you can get some serious practice for the answer about virtue.

[71]   MENO: No, but you say it, Socrates.   75B

[72]   SOCRATES: You want me to gratify you?

[73]   MENO: I certainly do.

[74]   SOCRATES: Will you then also be willing to tell me about virtue?

[75]   MENO: I will.

[76]   SOCRATES: Well then, one must be for it; for it is a worthy endeavor.

[77]   MENO: By all means.

[78]   SOCRATES: Come then, let us try to tell you what shape is. See then whether you can accept it to be the following: for us, indeed, let this be shape: it is that which alone, of all the things that are, which always happens to accompany color. Is that sufficient for you, or do you somehow seek it in some other way? For I would be content if you could tell me about virtue in this way.

75C

[79]   MENO: But this is really simple-minded, Socrates.

[80]   SOCRATES: How do you mean that?

[81]   MENO: That shape is, in some way, according to your argument, that which always accompanies color. Very well; but if, indeed, someone should declare that he does not know color but is at a loss about it in the same way that he is about shape, what do you suppose you would have answered him?

[82]   SOCRATES: The truth is what I would have answered. And if the questioner were one of those wise men with a bent for strife and contention, I would tell him, "That's what I said. And if I don't speak correctly, it's your task to take up the argument and refute it." But if, being friends as both I and you are now, they should want to have a discussion with one another, then surely a somehow more gentle and more dialectical way of answering is required. And it is perhaps more dialectical to answer not only with the truth, but also through those things which he who is being questioned could agree that he knows. I too, indeed, will try to speak to you in this way. For, tell me, is there something you call an end? I mean this sort of thing, like a limit or an extremity—all these, I say, are the same thing, though perhaps Prodicus would differ from us; but you, at any rate, do call something as having been limited or ended. This is the sort of thing I want to say, nothing fancy.

75D

75E

[83]   MENO: But I do so call it that, and I think I do understand what you mean.

[84] SOCRATES: And what then? Is there something you call a 76A plane surface, and something else again you call a solid, as, for example, in geometry?

[85] MENO: I do so call them.

[86] SOCRATES: Therefore, you could immediately understand what I mean about shape. For I say this about every shape: that at which the solid ends, that is shape; what I could say, in summing it up, is that shape is the limit of a solid.

[87] MENO: And about color, what do you say, Socrates?

[88] SOCRATES: You are outrageous, Meno. You pose troublesome problems for an old man to answer, but you yourself are unwilling to recollect and say whatever 76B Gorgias says virtue is.

[89] MENO: But whenever you tell me this, Socrates, I'll tell you that.

[90] SOCRATES: Even someone who is blindfolded could know, Meno, from conversing with you that you are handsome and still have lovers.

[91] MENO: Why indeed?

[92] SOCRATES: Because you do nothing but impose commands in your arguments, the very thing that spoiled people do, so as to tyrannize as long as they are in their prime. And at the same time it is likely that you've noticed about 76C me, that I have a weakness for beautiful people. So I will gratify you and I will answer.

[93] MENO: By all means then, gratify me.

[94] SOCRATES: Then do you want me to answer in the style of Gorgias, by which you might be, as much as possible, able to follow?

[95] MENO: I do want it. And why not?

[96] SOCRATES: Then don't you people say, as does Empedocles, that there are certain effluences from the things that are?

[97] MENO: Very much so.

[98] SOCRATES: And there are certain passageways into which and through which the effluences pass?

[99]   MENO: Yes, by all means.

76D   [100]   SOCRATES: And that some of the effluences fit some of the passageways and others are too small or too large?

[101]   MENO: That is so.

[102]   SOCRATES: Then there is also something that you call sight?

[103]   MENO: I do.

[104]   SOCRATES: From these very agreements, as Pindar says, "understand what I mean." For color is an effluence of shapes commensurate with sight and perceptible.

[105]   MENO: You seem to me, Socrates, to have put this answer in the best possible way.

[106]   SOCRATES: Perhaps because it was said in accordance with the way in which you have been habituated. At the same time, I suppose, you consider that from this you could
76E   also say what sound is, and smell, and many other things of this sort.

[107]   MENO: By all means.

[108]   SOCRATES: For it is a tragical answer, Meno, and therefore satisfies you more than the one about shape.

[109]   MENO: It does.

[110]   SOCRATES: But it is not better, son of Alexidemus, but, as I persuade myself, the other one is. And I think it would not seem so to you, if it were not necessary, as you were saying yesterday, for you to leave before the Mysteries, but were both to stay around and to be initiated.

77A   [111]   MENO: But I would stay around, Socrates, if you would tell me about many other such things.

[112]   SOCRATES: But I certainly will in no way fall short of zeal, both for your sake and for my own, in talking about such things; but I do fear that I will not be able to talk about many such. But come now, you too try to pay back your promise to me in saying about virtue as a whole, what it is, and stop making many out of one, as those who like to jeer say each time about those who break something, but rather, leaving it whole and healthy, tell me what virtue
77B   is. The patterns, at any rate, you have got from me.

[113]   MENO: Well then, it seems to me, Socrates, that virtue is just what the poet says, " both to rejoice and to be capable in beautiful things." I too say that this is virtue: to desire beautiful things and to be capable of providing them for oneself.

[114]   SOCRATES: Then do you mean that he who desires beautiful things is someone who desires good things?

[115]   MENO: Most certainly.

[116]   SOCRATES: Then are you saying that there are some people who desire bad things and others who desire good things? Does it not seem to you, my very good man, that everyone desires good things?   77C

[117]   MENO: Not to me.

[118]   SOCRATES: But some desire bad things?

[119]   MENO: Yes.

[120]   SOCRATES: Supposing that the bad things are good, you mean, or even, while recognizing that they are bad, they nevertheless do desire them?

[121]   MENO: Both, it seems to me.

[122]   SOCRATES: Then does it really seem to you, Meno, that someone who recognizes that the bad things are bad, nevertheless desires them?

[123]   MENO: Certainly.

[124]   SOCRATES: What do you mean by "desires"? That they should become his?

[125]   MENO: Become his; what else could it be?

[126]   SOCRATES: Does he believe that the bad things benefit him whose they become, or does he recognize that bad things harm him whom they come to be with?   77D

[127]   MENO: There are some who believe the bad things benefit, and others who recognize that they harm.

[128]   SOCRATES: Do those who believe that bad things benefit also seem to you to recognize that bad things are bad?

[129]   MENO: This does not seem to me to be so at all.

[130]   SOCRATES: Therefore it is clear that those who do not recognize bad things as bad do not desire bad things, but   77E

they desire those things which they were supposing to be good, the very things which are, in fact, bad; so that not recognizing bad things to be bad and supposing them to be good, it is clear that they desire good things. Is it not so?

[131]   MENO: These, at any rate, probably do.

[132]   SOCRATES: What then? Those who desire bad things, as you affirm, but who believe that the bad things harm him to whom they come to belong, they surely recognize that they are harmed by them?

78A   [133]   MENO: Necessarily.

[134]   SOCRATES: But do not these men think that those being harmed are miserable to the extent that they are being harmed?

[135]   MENO: This too is necessary.

[136]   SOCRATES: And are not the miserable ill-fated?

[137]   MENO: I, anyway, think they are.

[138]   SOCRATES: Now is there anyone who wishes to be miserable and ill-fated?

[139]   MENO: It does not seem so to me, Socrates.

[140]   SOCRATES: Therefore, no one, Meno, wishes for bad things, if indeed he does not wish to be this sort of person. For what else is it to be miserable than both to desire and to acquire bad things?

78B   [141]   MENO: I dare say you speak the truth, Socrates, and no one wishes bad things for himself.

[142]   SOCRATES: Then were you saying just now that virtue is to wish for good things and to be capable of them?

[143]   MENO: I sure did say it.

[144]   SOCRATES: Then from what has just been said, does not the wishing pertain to everyone, and in this respect no one is better than anyone else?

[145]   MENO: So it appears.

[146]   SOCRATES: But it is clear that if one man is better than another it would be by being more excellent in capability.

[147]   MENO: Certainly so.

[148]   SOCRATES: This, therefore, as it seems, is, according to your argument, virtue: a power of providing good things for oneself.   78C

[149]   MENO: It seems to me, Socrates, altogether to hold in just the way you now understand it.

[150]   SOCRATES: Now let us see in this, too, whether what you say is true, for you could perhaps be speaking well. Do you affirm that to be able to provide oneself with good things is virtue?

[151]   MENO: I do.

[152]   SOCRATES: Are not both health and wealth the kinds of things that you call goods?

[153]   MENO: And to acquire gold, I mean, and silver, and honors in a city and offices.

[154]   SOCRATES: You don't mean, I suppose, that some things other than this kind are the good things?

[155]   MENO: No, but I mean everything of this kind.   78D

[156]   SOCRATES: Very well; to provide oneself with gold and silver, then, is virtue, as declares Meno, the ancestral guest-friend of the Great King. Do you add the words "justly" and "piously" to this providing, Meno, or does it make no difference to you, but even if someone should provide himself with these things unjustly, would you still call these doings virtue?

[157]   MENO: Surely not, Socrates.

[158]   SOCRATES: But vice.

[159]   MENO: By all means, surely

[160]   SOCRATES: Therefore it seems likely that one should add justice or moderation or piety, or some other piece of virtue, to this providing. And, if not, it will not be virtue, even though it were a thoroughgoing provision of the good things.   78E

[161]   MENO: For how could virtue come to be without these things?

[162]   SOCRATES: And not procuring gold and silver, whenever it is not just, either for oneself or for another, is not this lack

of provision also virtue?

[163]   MENO: So it appears.

[164]   SOCRATES: Therefore, the providing of goods such as these could be virtue no more than the lack of a way of providing them; but it is likely that whatever comes about with justice will be virtue and that whatever comes about without anything of this sort will be vice.

79A

[165]   MENO: It seems to me that it must be necessarily as you say.

[166]   SOCRATES: Then did we not affirm a little while ago that each piece of these things was virtue, justice and moderation and everything of this sort?

[167]   MENO: Yes.

[168]   SOCRATES: So, Meno, are you making fun of me?

[169]   MENO: How indeed is that, Socrates?

[170]   SOCRATES: Because just now when you were requested by me not to shatter virtue or to change it into small coin, and I gave you patterns in accordance with which it was to be answered, yet you paid no attention to this and tell me that virtue is to be able to provide good things for oneself along with justice. And this, you declare, is a piece of virtue?

79B

[171]   MENO: I do.

[172]   SOCRATES: Then it follows from what you agree to, that to act, whatever one might do, with a piece of virtue, this is virtue. For you affirm that justice and each of these is a piece of virtue. Why then do I say this? Because when I begged you to talk about virtue as a whole, you fell far short of saying what it is, but you declared that every action is a virtue whenever it is done with some piece of virtue, just as if you had said what the whole, virtue, is and it was immediately recognized by me, even if you were to change it into pieces of small change. Now what you need, again from the beginning, it seems to me, my dear Meno, is the same question, What is virtue?—if every action with a piece of virtue could be virtue. For this is what it means whenever someone says that every action accompanied by justice is virtue. Does it not seem to you that the same question is required again, or do you rather suppose that someone knows what a piece of

79C

virtue is, without knowing virtue itself?

[173]   MENO: It does not seem so to me.

[174]   SOCRATES: For, if you also remember, when I had just   **79D**
        answered you about shape, we, I think, rejected the kind
        of answer that tries to answer through those things that
        are still being sought and are not yet agreed upon.

[175]   MENO: And we were right in rejecting it, Socrates.

[176]   SOCRATES: Therefore, my very good man, while what
        virtue is as a whole is still being sought, do not suppose
        that in answering through its pieces you will in any way
        clarify it, or anything else, by speaking of it in this same
        way, but consider that you will be in need again of the   **79E**
        very same question. What is this virtue that you speak
        about as you speak? Or does it seem to you that I'm not
        saying anything?

[177]   MENO: You seem to me to speak rightly.

[178]   SOCRATES: Then answer again, from the beginning: what
        do you affirm virtue to be, both you and your comrade?

[179]   MENO: Socrates, I certainly used to hear, even before
        meeting you, that you never do anything else than exist   **80A**
        in a state of perplexity yourself and put others in a state
        of perplexity. And now you seem to me to be bewitching
        me and drugging me and simply subduing me with
        incantations, so that I come to be full of perplexity.
        And you seem to me, if it is even appropriate to make
        something of a joke, to be altogether, both in looks and
        in other respects, like the flat torpedo-fish of the sea. For,
        indeed, it always makes anyone who approaches and
        touches it grow numb, and you seem to me now to have
        done that very sort of thing to me, making me numb. For
        truly, both in soul and in mouth, I am numb and have   **80B**
        nothing with which I can answer you. And yet thousands
        of times I have made a great many speeches about virtue,
        and before many people, and done very well, in my own
        opinion anyway; yet now I'm altogether unable to say
        what it is. And it seems to me that you are well-advised
        not to sail away or emigrate from here: for, if you, a
        foreigner in a different city, were to do this sort of thing,
        you would probably be arrested as a sorcerer.

[180]   SOCRATES: You are a clever rogue, Meno, and you almost
        deceived me.

[181]   MENO: What are you getting at, Socrates?

80C   [182]   SOCRATES: I'm aware of why you portrayed me in a likeness.

[183]   MENO: Why, indeed, do you suppose?

[184]   SOCRATES: So that I would make a likeness of you in return. And I know this about all beautiful people, that they delight in having images made of them; it pays for them. Because, I suppose, even the images of beautiful people are beautiful. But I will not make an image of you in return. And I—if the torpedo-fish itself is numb in its way even as it also makes others numb—I am like it: but if not, not. For it is not while being well-provided myself that I make others unprovided or perplexed; but it is while I myself, more than anyone, am unprovided or perplexed, that I make others unprovided or perplexed. And now about virtue, I do not know what it is; but you, of course, perhaps, did know it earlier, before you came into contact with me, but now you are certainly like one who does not know. Nevertheless, I am willing to look with you and seek together for whatever it is.

80D

[185]   MENO: And in what way will you seek, Socrates, for that which you know nothing at all about what it is? What sort of thing among those things which you do not know are you proposing to seek for yourself? Or, even if, at best, you should happen upon it, how will you know it is that which you did not know?

80E   [186]   SOCRATES: I understand the sort of thing you want to say, Meno. Do you not see how inclined to strife this argument you are drawing out is, that it is not possible for a human being to seek either what he knows or what he does not know? For he could not seek for what he knows, because he knows it and then there's no need of any seeking for this sort of person; nor could he seek for what he does not know, because then he does not know what he is seeking.

81A   [187]   MENO: Doesn't this argument seem to you to have been said beautifully, Socrates?

[188]   SOCRATES: No, not to me.

[189]   MENO: Can you say in what way?

[190]   SOCRATES: I can. For I have heard from both men and

women wise about things divine–

[191] MENO: What was the account they gave?

[192] SOCRATES: A true one, it seems to me, and a beautiful one.

[193] MENO: What is it, and who are those who say it?

[194] SOCRATES: Those who say it are among those priests and priestesses who have made it their concern to be able to give an account about those things they have taken in hand. And Pindar speaks too and many others of those **81B** poets who are divine. And what they say is this– but look whether they seem to you to speak the truth– for they declare the human soul to be immortal, and that at one time it comes to an end, which indeed they call dying, and again, at another time, it comes into being, but it is never destroyed. Indeed, because of this, one is required to live through one's life as piously as possible. "For those from whom

> Persephone has accepted redemption for the ancient affliction, of these in the ninth year she sends the souls above again to the upper sun. From them glorious kings grow up, men with sweeping strength **81C** and greatest wisdom, and for the rest of time they are called holy heroes by mankind.

Inasmuch as the soul is immortal and has been born many times and has seen all things both here and in the house of Hades, there is nothing which it has not learned. So that there is nothing wondrous about its also being able to recollect about virtue and about other things, which it already knew before. For inasmuch as all nature is akin and the soul has learned all things, there is nothing **81D** to prevent someone who recollects (which people call learning) one thing only from discovering all other things, so long as he is brave and does not grow tired of seeking. For seeking and learning therefore consist wholly in recollection. So then one must not be persuaded by this contentious argument. For it would make us lazy and is pleasant only for fainthearted people to hear, but the other argument makes us both ready to work and to seek. **81E** Trusting in this one to be true, I am willing with you to seek for whatever virtue is.

[195] MENO: Yes, Socrates. But how do you mean this: that we do

not learn, but that what we call learning is recollection? Can you teach me how this can be?

82A [196] SOCRATES: And after I just now said, Meno, that you are a clever rogue, you ask me now if I can teach you—I who deny that teaching is anything but recollection—in order that I may straightway be shown up to be contradicting myself.

[197] MENO: No, by Zeus, Socrates, I was not looking to that when I spoke, but it was just by habit. But if you somehow can point out to me that it is as you say, point it out.

[198] SOCRATES: But it's not easy, nevertheless I'm willing to make the effort for your sake. But call over one of these **82B** many followers of yours here for me, whichever you want, so that in him I'll be able to exhibit things for you.

[199] MENO: By all means. You, come here.

[200] SOCRATES: He is Greek, then, and speaks Greek?

[201] MENO: By all means, very much so; he was born in the house.

[202] SOCRATES: Now then turn your mind to which of the two ways he seems to you to exhibit, recollecting or learning from me.

[203] MENO: Of course, I'll turn my mind to it.

[204] SOCRATES: Now tell me, Boy, do you know that a square area is this sort of thing? [*Figure 1*]

[205] BOY: I do.

82C [206] SOCRATES: Then a square area has all these lines, being four in number, equal? [*Figure 1*]

[207] BOY: Certainly.

[208] SOCRATES: Does it not also have these lines here, through the middle [of each side of the square] equal? [*Figure 2*]

[209] BOY: Yes.

[210] SOCRATES: Then could not this sort of area be larger or smaller?

[211] BOY: Certainly.

[212] SOCRATES: If then this side were two feet and this other side two feet, how many feet would the whole be? [*Figure*

3] Look at it this way: if this side were two feet and this other side only one foot, would not the area be once times two feet? [*Figure 4*]

[213] BOY: Yes.

[214] SOCRATES: But as this other side is also two feet [*Figure 5*], does it not become twice two? [*Figure 6*] **82D**

[215] BOY: It does.

[216] SOCRATES: Therefore, it becomes two times two feet?

[217] BOY: Yes.

[218] SOCRATES: How many, then, are the two times two feet? After you have calculated it, tell me.

[219] BOY: Four, Socrates. [*Figure 7*]

[220] SOCRATES: Then could there not come to be another area two times as large as this one, and of the same sort, having all its lines equal, just as this one? [*Figure 8*]

[221] BOY: Yes.

[222] SOCRATES: How many feet, then, will it be?

[223] BOY: Eight.

[224] SOCRATES: Come then, try to tell me how large each line of that area will be. For the line of this one is two feet. [*Figure 9*] What then is the line of that area two times as large? **82E**

[225] BOY: It is clear, Socrates, that the line is two times as large.

[226] SOCRATES: Do you see, Meno, that I am not teaching him anything, but all that I do is ask questions? And now he supposes that he knows what sort of line it is from which the eight-foot area will come to be. Or does it not seem so to you?

[227] MENO: It does to me.

[228] SOCRATES: Does he know then?

[229] MENO: Surely not.

[230] SOCRATES: For he supposes that it comes from the double line?

[231] MENO: Yes.

[232] SOCRATES: Watch him now recollecting in order, just as one should recollect.

83A

And you, [Boy,] tell me: do you affirm that from the double line the double area comes to be? I mean this sort of thing: let it be an area that is not long on this side and short on the other, but equal on every side, just like this one here [*Figure 10*], and the double of this area, that is, an eight-foot area. But see if it still seems to you that it will be that from the double line.

[233]   BOY: It does to me.

[234]   SOCRATES: Then does this line become double of that if we add another of the same length here? [*Figure 11*]

[235]   BOY: Certainly.

[236]   SOCRATES: From this line then, you affirm, there will be the eight-foot area, whenever four lines of that length come

83B

to be? [*Figure 11*]

[237]   BOY: Yes.

[238]   SOCRATES: Then let us fill out the drawing from this line with four equal lines. [*Figure 12*] Then would not this one here be what you affirm is the eight-foot area? [*Figure 13*]

[239]   BOY: Certainly.

[240]   SOCRATES: Then in this one here there are four areas [*Figure 14*], each of which is equal to this four-foot area? [*Figure 15*]

[241]   BOY: Yes.

[242]   SOCRATES: How many then does it become? Is it not four times as great?

[243]   BOY: How not?

[244]   SOCRATES: Then is the area which is four times as great a double-area?

[245]   BOY: No, by Zeus!

[246]   SOCRATES: But how many times as much is it?

[247]   BOY: Four times as much.

[248]   SOCRATES: Therefore, Boy, from the double line, not the double area, but the fourfold area comes into being.

83C

[249]   BOY: You speak the truth.

[250]   SOCRATES: For four times an area of four feet is sixteen feet.

Isn't it?

[251] BOY: Yes. [*Figure 16*]

[252] SOCRATES: And from what sort of line does the eight-foot area come to be? Doesn't the fourfold area come from this line? [*Figure 17*]

[253] BOY: I say so.

[254] SOCRATES: And the four-foot area came from this half-line right here? [*Figure 18*]

[255] BOY: Yes.

[256] SOCRATES: Very well. Is not the eight-foot area double of this one [*Figure 19*] and half of that one [*Figure 20*]? Will it not be from a line greater than this one [*Figure 21*] but less than this one here [*Figure 22*]? Or not?

[257] BOY: It seems so to me.   83d

[258] SOCRATES: Fine. Keep answering this very thing, what seems so to you. And tell me, is not this line, as we said, two feet [*Figure 23*] and that line four [*Figure 24*]?

[259] BOY: Yes.

[260] SOCRATES: It must be, therefore, that the line of the eight-foot area is greater than this two-foot line [*Figure 25*], but less than the four-foot line [*Figure 26*].

[261] BOY: It must.

[262] SOCRATES: Try now to say what size you affirm it to be.   83e

[263] BOY: Three feet.

[264] SOCRATES: Then if it is to be three feet, let's take of this line [*Figure 27*] one half in addition [*Figure 28*] and it will be three feet [*Figure 29*]? For the feet of this one [*Figure 30*] is two and that of the other [*Figure 31*] is one; and the same way here these are two [*Figure 32*] and the other is one [*Figure 33*]; and this area of which you spoke comes into being. [*Figure 34*]

[265] BOY: Yes.

[266] SOCRATES: Then whenever it is three feet this way [*Figure 35*] and three feet that way [*Figure 36*], does the whole area become three times three feet? [*Figure 37*]

[267] BOY: It appears so.

[268]   SOCRATES: And how many feet are three times three?

[269]   BOY: Nine. [*Figure 38*]

[270]   SOCRATES: And how many feet was the required double area to be?

[271]   BOY: Eight.

[272]   SOCRATES: Therefore, in no way does the eight-foot area come to be from the three-feet line. [*Figure 39*]

[273]   BOY: Surely not.

84A

[274]   SOCRATES: But from what sort of line? Try to tell us precisely: and if you don't want to count, show us rather, from what sort of line.

[275]   BOY: But, by Zeus, Socrates, I, for one, do not know.

84B

[276]   SOCRATES: Are you considering again, Meno, how far it is that he has now gone in his recollecting? That, at first, he did not know what the line of the eight-foot area is, just as now he does not yet know, but, however that may be, then he thought he knew it, and boldly answered as one who knows, and he did not believe that he was unprovided and perplexed. But now, at this time, he believes that he is unprovided and perplexed, and just as he does not know, he does not think that he knows.

[277]   MENO: You speak the truth.

[278]   SOCRATES: Then is he not better off now, about the thing which he did not know?

[279]   MENO: This too seems to me so.

[280]   SOCRATES: Then by making him unprovided and perplexed and numbing him, just like the torpedo-fish, have we in any way harmed him?

[281]   MENO: It does not seem so to me.

84C

[282]   SOCRATES: Then, at any rate, we have done something useful for the work at hand, as is fitting for discovering how things are. For now he, not knowing, can even carry on the search gladly, whereas then he could easily think that both before many people and many times he could speak well about the double area, how it required having the line that was double in length.

[283]   MENO: It seems likely.

[284]   SOCRATES: Well, do you think that before he would have tried to seek for or to learn that which he thought he knew while he did not know—before he fell down into perplexity and want and came to believe that he did not know, and longed to know?

[285]   MENO: It does not seem so to me, Socrates.

[286]   SOCRATES: Did he benefit, then, from being numbed?

[287]   MENO: It seems so to me.

[288]   SOCRATES: Look, now, at what he will discover from this perplexity and want, searching along with me, while I do nothing but ask questions and do not teach. And watch out for whether you might discover me somehow   **84D** teaching and explaining things to him instead of asking for his own opinions about the matter.

　　　　　For you, [Boy,] tell me: Is not this our four-foot area? [*Figure 40*] Do you understand?

[289]   BOY: I do.

[290]   SOCRATES: And can we not add here another area equal to it? [*Figure 41*]

[291]   BOY: Yes.

[292]   SOCRATES: And this third one equal to each of these? [*Figure 42*]

[293]   BOY: Yes.

[294]   SOCRATES: Then can we add this one in the corner so as to fill it out? [*Figure 43*]

[295]   BOY: Certainly.

[296]   SOCRATES: Then would it not come about that there are   **84e** these four equal areas? [*Figure 44*]

[297]   BOY: Yes.

[298]   SOCRATES: What then? How many times more does this whole area [*Figure 45*] become than that one [*Figure 46*]?

[299]   BOY: Four times.

[300]   SOCRATES: But what we needed was the double area. Or don't you remember?

[301]   BOY: I certainly do.

[302]   SOCRATES: Is this not, then, a line [*Figure 47*] going from
85A   corner to corner [*Figure 48*], and cutting each of these
        areas in two [*Figure 49*]?

[303]   BOY: Yes.

[304]   SOCRATES: Then do not these four equal lines come about
        containing this area here? [*Figure 50*]

[305]   BOY: They sure do.

[306]   SOCRATES: Look now: what size is this area?

[307]   BOY: I don't understand.

[308]   SOCRATES: Has not each of these inside lines [*Figures 51,
        52*] cut off half of each of these four areas [*Figure 53*]? Or
        not?

[309]   BOY: Yes.

[310]   SOCRATES: Then how many areas of this size [*Figure 54*] are
        there in this area? [*Figure 55*]

[311]   BOY: Four. [*Figure 56*]

[312]   SOCRATES: And how many in this area here? [*Figure 57*]

[313]   BOY: Two. [*Figure 58*]

[314]   SOCRATES: And what is the relation of the four to the two?

[315]   BOY: Double.

[316]   SOCRATES: Then how many feet does this area become?
85B   [*Figure 59*]

[317]   BOY: Eight feet. [*Figures 60, 61*]

[318]   SOCRATES: From what kind of line?

[319]   BOY: From this one. [*Figure 62*]

[320]   SOCRATES: From the one stretching from corner to corner
        of the four-foot area? [*Figure 63*]

[321]   BOY: Yes.

[322]   SOCRATES: The Sophists call this line the diagonal; so that
        if diagonal is its name, it would be from the diagonal,
        as you, Meno's boy, declare, that the double area would
        come to be. [*Figure 64*]

[323]   BOY: By all means, Socrates.

[324] SOCRATES: What does it seem to you, Meno? Is there any opinion which he gave in his answers that was not his own?

[325] MENO: No, they were all his own.   85C

[326] SOCRATES: And yet he did not know, as we were saying a little while ago.

[327] MENO: You speak the truth.

[328] SOCRATES: Still, these opinions were in him, were they not?

[329] MENO: Yes.

[330] SOCRATES: Then in someone who does not know about that which he does not know, there are true opinions about those things which he does not know?

[331] MENO: So it appears.

[332] SOCRATES: And now those very opinions have just been stirred up in him, like a dream. But if someone were to ask him these same questions many times and in different ways, you know that he will finally understand them no less precisely than anyone else.   85D

[333] MENO: It seems likely.

[334] SOCRATES: Then with no one teaching, but someone only asking questions, he will understand, he himself taking up the knowledge again out of himself?

[335] MENO: Yes.

[336] SOCRATES: And his taking up knowledge again that is in himself, is this not recollecting?

[337] MENO: Certainly.

[338] SOCRATES: Then concerning the knowledge which he now has, is it not either that at some time he acquired it or that he always had it?

[339] MENO: Yes.

[340] SOCRATES: Then if he always had it, he was also always one who knows; but, if he acquired it at some time, he could not have acquired it in his present life. Or has someone taught him how to do geometry? For then he   85E will do these same things with all of geometry and all the other subjects of learning. Is there then any one who has

taught him all these things? For you, I guess, are just the man to know, especially since he was born and raised in your house.

[341]   MENO: But I know that no one ever taught him.

[342]   SOCRATES: Does he have these opinions or not?

[343]   MENO: Necessarily, Socrates, it appears so.

86A

[344]   SOCRATES: But if he did not acquire them in his present life, is this not now clear that he had them and learned them in some other time?

[345]   MENO: So it appears.

[346]   SOCRATES: Then was this the time when he was not a human being?

[347]   MENO: Yes.

[348]   SOCRATES: If then both during the time in which he is and the time in which he is not a human being, true opinions will exist within him, which after being aroused by questioning become matters of knowledge, then will not his soul for all time be in a condition of having learned? For it is clear that for all time he is, or he is not, a human being.

[349]   MENO: So it appears.

86B   [350]   SOCRATES: Then if the truth about the things which are is always in our soul, the soul would be immortal, so that you must be bold about what you now happen not to know, that is, what is not remembered, to try to seek and to recollect it?

[351]   MENO: You seem to me to speak well, Socrates, I don't know how.

[352]   SOCRATES: And so do I to myself, Meno. And for the rest of the points I would not assert myself altogether confidently on behalf of my argument; but that in supposing one ought to seek what one does not know we would be better, more able to be brave and less lazy than if we supposed that which we do not know we are neither capable of discovering nor ought to seek—on behalf of that I would surely battle, so far as I am able, both in word and in deed.

86C

[353]   MENO: That, too, you seem to me to speak well, Socrates.

[354] SOCRATES: Do you want us, then, since we are of one mind that one ought to seek for what one does not know, to try to seek in common for what virtue is?

[355] MENO: By all means. Not, Socrates, but that I would with most pleasure both look for and hear about that which I asked about at first, whether one ought to undertake it as being itself teachable, or as by nature, or as in whatever way virtue comes to human beings. **86D**

[356] SOCRATES: Yet, Meno, if I were ruling not only myself, but you too, we would not first look at whether virtue is something teachable or not teachable before we first sought what it itself is: but, since you don't even try to rule yourself, in order indeed that you might be free, you both try to rule me and do rule me, I will yield to you— for what can I do? It seems, then, that we must look into **86E** what sort of thing something is, something about which we don't yet know what it is. If you won't do anything else, at least relax your rule a little for me and agree to examine it hypothetically, whether it is teachable or whatever. And I mean by "hypothetically" the following: just as geometers often look at things whenever someone asks them, for example, about a figure, whether this triangular figure is able to be inscribed in this circle, **87A** someone might say: "I don't yet know if this is that sort of figure, but I think I have, as it were, a certain hypothesis useful for the problem, as follows: If this is the sort of figure which, after someone applies it to the given line of itself, falls short by that sort of figure like the one which has been itself applied, then one thing seems to me to result; and some other thing results if, on the other hand, it is impossible for this to fall out. So then it is on the **87B** hypothesis of the inscription of the figure in the circle that I am willing to tell you whether the result is impossible or not." In this way then, about virtue too—since we know neither what it is, nor what sort of thing it is—let us look hypothetically at it, whether it is teachable or not teachable, speaking in the following way: If virtue is some sort of thing among those things that have regard to the soul, would it be teachable or not teachable? First, then, if it's the kind of thing that is different from, or like, knowledge, is it teachable or not, or, as we were just now saying it, is it recollectable?—let it make no difference to **87C** us about whatever name we use—but is it teachable? Or is this, at any rate, clear to everyone, that a human being

is taught nothing else than knowledge?

[357]   MENO: It seems so to me.

[358]   SOCRATES: And if virtue is some kind of knowledge, it is clear that it could be taught.

[359]   MENO: For how not?

[360]   SOCRATES: Well, we are rid of this quickly, that if virtue is one sort of thing it is teachable, if it is another sort, it is not.

[361]   MENO: Certainly.

[362]   SOCRATES: And after this, it seems likely, that whether virtue is knowledge or the kind of thing that is different from knowledge should be looked into.

87D   [363]   MENO: It seems to me, anyway, that this should be looked into after that.

[364]   SOCRATES: Well, what then? Do we not affirm that virtue is a good thing in itself, and does this same hypothesis remain with us, that it is a good thing in itself?

[365]   MENO: By all means.

[366]   SOCRATES: Then, if there is something good and it is something else separated from knowledge, it may be that virtue would not be some sort of knowledge; but if there is nothing good which knowledge does not encompass, then we would be right in suspecting what we suspected, that it is some sort of knowledge.

[367]   MENO: That is so.

87E   [368]   SOCRATES: And surely it is by means of virtue that we are good?

[369]   MENO: Yes.

[370]   SOCRATES: And if we are good, we are beneficent: for all good things are beneficial. Are they not?

[371]   MENO: Yes.

[372]   SOCRATES: Now virtue, too, is beneficial?

[373]   MENO: Necessarily, from what has been agreed to.

[374]   SOCRATES: Now let us see, taking them up one by one, what sorts of things are beneficial for us: health, we affirm, and

strength, and beauty and, surely, wealth: these and these kinds of things we say are beneficial. Do we not?

[375]   MENO: Yes.   88A

[376]   SOCRATES: But these same things, we affirm, sometimes also harm; or do you affirm it otherwise than this?

[377]   MENO: No, but this way.

[378]   SOCRATES: Now look, what directs each of these things whenever it benefits us and whenever it harms? Then is it not that whenever right usage directs, it benefits; but when not, it harms?

[379]   MENO: Certainly.

[380]   SOCRATES: Now, then, let us look also at those things that pertain to the soul. Is there something that you call moderation, as well as justice and courage and readiness-to-learn and memory and magnificence, and all such kinds of things?

[381]   MENO: I do.

[382]   SOCRATES: Now look at whether any of these things seem   88B to you to be not knowledge, but something other than knowledge; whether they don't sometimes harm and sometimes benefit? For example, courage, if the courage is not prudence, but some sort of boldness—is it not the case that when a human being is bold without intelligence that he is harmed and whenever with intelligence he is benefited?

[383]   MENO: Yes.

[384]   SOCRATES: Then is it also the same with moderation and readiness to learn; when they are learned and trained for with intelligence, they are beneficial, but without intelligence, harmful?

[385]   MENO: Very much so.

[386]   SOCRATES: Then, in sum, all the things undertaken and   88C endured by the soul when directed by prudence come to end in happiness, but when controlled by thoughtlessness in the opposite?

[387]   MENO: It seems likely.

[388]   SOCRATES: If then virtue is something in the soul and is itself necessarily beneficial, it must be prudence:

88D

since, indeed, all things that pertain to the soul are, themselves in themselves neither beneficial nor harmful, but when prudence or thoughtlessness is added to them, they become harmful or beneficial. According to this argument, indeed, virtue being beneficial, it must be some kind of prudence.

[389]   MENO: It seems so to me.

[390]   SOCRATES: And plainly also the other things we were just now talking about, wealth and those kinds of things, are sometimes good and sometimes harmful. Then just as prudence directing the rest of the soul makes the things of the soul beneficial and thoughtlessness makes them harmful, in this way again does not the soul, by rightly using and directing these things too, make them beneficial, but if not rightly makes them harmful?

[391]   MENO: Certainly.

[392]   SOCRATES: And does the thoughtful soul direct rightly, but the thoughtless mistakenly?

[393]   MENO: That is so.

89A

[394]   SOCRATES: Then is it possible to speak in just this way about everything, that for a human being all other things depend upon the soul, but the things of the soul itself depend upon prudence, if they are going to be good: and by this argument the beneficial would be prudence: and do we affirm that virtue is beneficial?

[395]   MENO: Certainly.

[396]   SOCRATES: Therefore, do we affirm that prudence is virtue, either virtue altogether or some part of it?

[397]   MENO: It seems to me, Socrates, that the things which have been said have been finely said.

[398]   SOCRATES: Then if this is how it is, the good could not be good by nature.

[399]   MENO: It doesn't seem so to me.

89B   [400]   SOCRATES: For even if this somehow were so, this too would follow: if the good were to become so by nature, we would, I guess, have people who recognized those among the youth with good natures, whom, after we took them from those who had revealed them, we would guard on the Acropolis, setting our seal on them much more than we do with gold, so that no one could corrupt them, and that when they should come of age, they could become useful to their cities.

[401]   MENO: That is surely likely, Socrates.

[402]   SOCRATES: Since, then, the good become good not by nature, then is it by learning?   **89C**

[403]   MENO: It now seems to me to be necessary: and it is clear, Socrates, according to the hypothesis, that if virtue is indeed knowledge, it is teachable.

[404]   SOCRATES: Perhaps, by Zeus; but maybe we did not agree rightly about this?

[405]   MENO: And yet it did seem just now to have been said rightly.

[406]   SOCRATES: But it ought not to seem to have been said rightly only just now, but also in the present time and in the time to come, if there's going to be some soundness about it.

[407]   MENO: What then is this? What are you seeing that   **89D** bothers you about it and makes you doubt that virtue is knowledge?

[408]   SOCRATES: I will tell you, Meno. For that it is teachable, if, indeed, it is knowledge, I don't take back as not being said rightly; but that it may not be knowledge, see whether I seem to you to be reasonable in my doubt about that. For tell me this: if anything whatever is teachable, and not only virtue, are there not necessarily also teachers and learners of it?

[409]   MENO: It seems so to me.

[410]   SOCRATES: Then, again, on the contrary, that of which   **89E** there would be neither teachers nor learners, would we not liken it rightly if we should liken it to what is not teachable?

[411]   MENO: That is so. But does it seem to you that there are no teachers of virtue?

[412]   SOCRATES: I've sought, surely, many times, whether there might be some teachers of it and, trying everything, I'm not able to find out. And yet I share the search with many people, and especially those whom I suppose to be most experienced in this matter. And now indeed, Meno, just at

the right moment, Anytus here has sat down beside us, to whom we should give a share in the search. And it would

90A

be fitting for us to give him a share: for Anytus here, first of all, is the son of a father both wealthy and wise, Anthemion, who became wealthy not by chance, nor from some gift, like the one who has just recently received Polycrates' goods, Ismenias the Theban, but acquired it by his own wisdom and diligence. Then, in other respects too, he did not seem to be a haughty citizen, nor puffed-up and offensive, but an orderly and well-mannered man.

90B

Then he brought up and educated our man here well, as the majority of the Athenians judge; they elect him, at any rate, to the highest offices. Now it is only just to search for teachers of virtue with such men, whether there are or are not any and whoever they might be.

You, then, Anytus, do search along with us, both with me and your guest-friend, Meno, here, whether in this matter there might be any teachers. And look at it this way: if we should want Meno here to become a good doctor, to whom would we send him as teachers? Would

90C

it not be to the doctors?

[413]   ANYTUS: Certainly.

[414]   SOCRATES: And what if we should want him to become a good shoemaker, would we not send him to the shoemakers?

[415]   ANYTUS: Yes.

[416]   SOCRATES: So, too, with the others?

[417]   ANYTUS: Certainly.

[418]   SOCRATES: Now tell me again about these same cases, in this way. To the doctors, we say, we would send him rightly, if we were to send him, wanting him to become a doctor. Now whenever we say that, do we also say this, that we would be sensible, if we sent him to those who

90D

claim to practice the art, rather than to those who don't, and because they practice the art charge fees for it, who have declared themselves to be teachers for anyone who wants to come and learn? Then, if we had looked to these things, would we not be right in sending him?

[419]   ANYTUS: Yes.

[420]   SOCRATES: Then do not these same things hold for flute-playing and the rest? It's very foolish of those who want **90E** to make someone a flute-player to be unwilling to send him to those who undertake to teach the art and who charge a fee for it, but who make trouble by having the student seek to learn from those who neither pretend to be teachers nor have any student in that very subject which we consider the one for which we would send someone to learn from them. Does this not seem very unreasonable to you?

[421]   ANYTUS: Yes, by Zeus, to me it does, and stupid as well.

[422]   SOCRATES: Finely spoken. Then now it should be possible for you to deliberate in common with me about this **91A** guest-friend of ours, Meno here. For he, Anytus, has been saying to me for some time now that he desires that wisdom and virtue by which people manage both households and cities finely, and take care of their own parents, and know how to receive and to send off both citizens and foreigners hospitably, in a way worthy of a good man. Then in order to learn this virtue, consider to whom, if we sent him, we would rightly send him. Or, is **91B** it clear, indeed, according to the argument just made, it should be to those who undertake to be teachers of virtue and have professed themselves publicly to any Greek who wants to learn, and have fixed fees that they charge for it?

[423]   ANYTUS: And just who are these people you speak of, Socrates?

[424]   SOCRATES: Surely you too know that these are those whom people call Sophists.

[425]   ANYTUS: By Heracles, watch what you're saying, Socrates. **91C** May such madness not seize any of my own people, neither my family nor my friends, neither fellow-citizen nor foreigner, so as to be debased by going to them, since it is evident that these men are the debasement and corruption of those who associate with them.

[426]   SOCRATES: How do you mean that, Anytus? Then do these alone of those who claim to know some way of doing good differ by so much from the others, that they not only do not benefit whatever one hands over to them, but even, on the contrary, ruin it? And for these services they **91D** openly consider themselves entitled to demand money?

Now I cannot believe you: for I know one man, Protagoras, who acquired more money from this wisdom of his than Phidias, who produced such manifestly beautiful works, and any ten other sculptors. And yet how portentous what you say is, considering that those who work on old shoes and mend clothes would not be able to get away, for thirty days, with giving back the clothes and shoes in more miserable condition than they received them, but if they ever did such things, they would soon die of hunger. And yet Protagoras hid it from the whole of Greece for forty years that he was corrupting his associates and sending them back more miserable than he received them. For I think when he died he was nearly seventy years old, after being in his art for forty years. And in all this time, up to this very day, he has not ceased to be well thought of; and not only Protagoras, but very many others as well, some born before him and others still alive now. Then, indeed, should we declare, according to your argument, that they knowingly deceived and ruined the youth, or that it had been hidden from themselves too? And shall we deem those whom some declare to be the wisest of human beings to be so mad?

[427]   ANYTUS: They are far from being mad, Socrates; but much more so are the youth who give them money, and even more than these are the relatives who turn them over to them, but most of all are the cities that permit them to come in and don't drive them out, whether it's some foreigner that undertakes to do something of this sort, or a fellow citizen.

[428]   SOCRATES: Has any one of the Sophists wronged you, Anytus, that you should be so hard on them?

[429]   ANYTUS: No, by Zeus, I never associated with any of them, and I would not allow anyone else of my people to do so.

[430]   SOCRATES: Then you are altogether without experience of these men?

[431]   ANYTUS: I am and may I remain so.

[432]   SOCRATES: How then, my daemonic one, could you know about this business, whether there is anything good or worthless in that of which you are altogether without experience?

91E

92A

92B

92C

[433]   ANYTUS: Easily: I still know what these people are, whether I am without experience of them or not.

[434]   SOCRATES: You are perhaps a diviner, Anytus, for how else, I might wonder, do you know about them, from what you yourself say about them. But we are not searching for those from whose company Meno would become worthless after he came to them,—for these, if you want, let them be the Sophists—but tell us, and do your hereditary comrade here a good turn by telling him, to whom to go in so great a city as this so that he might become worthy of mention in the virtue I was just now going through.   **92D**

[435]   ANYTUS: Why don't you tell him?

[436]   SOCRATES: Well, I did say who I thought were teachers of these things; but it happened that I made no sense, as you say. And perhaps there is something to what you say. But you now, in your turn, tell him to whom among the Athenians he should go. Tell him the name of anyone you want.   **92E**

[437]   ANYTUS: Why should one hear the name of just one man? For of any Athenian gentleman he should happen to meet, there is none who will not make him better than the Sophists would, if he is willing to listen.

[438]   SOCRATES: Did these gentlemen become such spontaneously, and yet without learning from anyone are they nevertheless able to teach others what they themselves did not learn?   **93A**

[439]   ANYTUS: I claim that they too learned from those who were gentlemen before them: or don't you think that there have been many good men in this city?

[440]   SOCRATES: I, too, do think, Anytus, that there are good men in politics here, and before now there have been men no worse than they are, but have they also been good teachers of this virtue of theirs? For this is what our discussion happens to be about: not whether or not there are good men here, nor whether there have been such before, but we have for some time been looking into whether virtue is teachable. And in looking into this, we look into the following, whether the good men, both those now and those before, knew how to hand over to another the virtue in which they were good, or whether   **93B**

this is not something able to be handed over or to be received by any human being from another. This is what I and Meno have for some time been seeking. Now, look at it this way, out of your own argument: would you not affirm that Themistocles was a good man?

93C

[441]   ANYTUS: I would, even the best of all.

[442]   SOCRATES: And therefore that he was a good teacher, if anyone was a teacher of his own virtue?

[443]   ANYTUS: I suppose so, if he wanted to be.

[444]   SOCRATES: But do you think that he would not have wanted any others to become gentlemen, and especially his own son? Or do you think he begrudged him getting it, and purposely did not pass on the virtue in which he himself was good? Or haven't you heard that Themistocles had his son Cleophantus taught to be a good horseman. He could even stay on horses while standing upright and hurl javelins from horses while upright; and he accomplished many other marvelous things in which his father had him educated and made him skilled; there were so many things for which he depended on good teachers. Haven't you heard about them from your elders?

93D

[445]   ANYTUS: I've heard.

[446]   SOCRATES: So then no one could have charged his son with having a nature that was bad.

93E   [447]   ANYTUS: Perhaps not.

[448]   SOCRATES: And what about this? Have you ever heard from anyone, either young or old, that Cleophantus, the son of Themistocles, became a good and wise man in those very things in which his father did?

[449]   ANYTUS: Surely not.

[450]   SOCRATES: Then are we to suppose that he wanted to educate his son in those other things, but in that wisdom in which he was himself wise, not to make him any better than his neighbors, if indeed virtue really is, as we were saying, teachable?

[451]   ANYTUS: Perhaps not, by Zeus.

[452]   SOCRATES: Here then is just such a teacher of virtue, whom you also agree to be among the best of those from former times. But let us look into another one, Aristides, the son

94A

of Lysimachus. Do you not agree that he was good?

[453]   ANYTUS: I certainly do, in every way.

[454]   SOCRATES: Then did he too not give his son, Lysimachus, the finest education of the Athenians, in all those things for which he had teachers, and does he seem to you to have made him a better man than anyone else? For you, I suppose, have been in his company, and see what sort of man he is. And, if you want, there is Pericles, so **94B** magnificently wise a man; do you know that he brought up two sons, Paralus and Xanthippus?

[455]   ANYTUS: I do.

[456]   SOCRATES: He certainly taught them, as you also know, to be no worse horsemen than any Athenian, and educated them in music and gymnastics and everything else that could be had by art to be inferior to no one; and did he not want to make them good men? I would think he wanted to, but it was not something teachable. And lest you think that only a few and the lowest Athenians are incapable **94C** in this affair, consider that Thucydides also brought up two sons, Melesias and Stephanus, and he educated them well both in other things and to be the finest wrestlers in Athens—he turned over the one to Xanthias, and the other to Eudorus; and they were, I guess, reputed to be the finest wrestlers of that time—or don't you remember?

[457]   ANYTUS: I do, by hearsay.

[458]   SOCRATES: Then is it clear that he would never, on the one hand, where it was required to go to considerable expense **94D** to teach, teach his own sons those things; but, on the other hand, where it was not required to spend a lot of money, to make them good men, fail to teach them, if that was something teachable? Or perhaps Thucydides was a low person and did not have many friends among Athenians and the allies? Yet he was from a great house and capable of great things in his city and among the other Greeks, so that if this thing were teachable, he would have found out who was going to make his sons good, either one of his countrymen, or some foreigner, if he himself had no **94E** leisure time because of his tending to the city. But, I fear, Anytus, my comrade, that virtue may not be something teachable.

[459]   ANYTUS: Socrates, it seems to me that you easily speak badly of people. Now I could give you some advice, if

95A

you're willing to be persuaded by me, to be careful: since it is perhaps easier to do harm to people than to benefit them in other cities too, and in this city that is certainly so. But I suppose you know that yourself.

[460]   SOCRATES: Meno, Anytus seems angry to me, and I don't wonder at it: for, first of all, he supposes me to be speaking badly about those men, and then he also believes himself to be one of them. But if he should ever know what sort of thing talking badly is, he will cease being angry, yet now he does not know. But you, tell me, are there not men among your people who are gentlemen too?

[461]   MENO: Certainly.

95B   [462]   SOCRATES: What then? Are these men willing to offer themselves as teachers to the youth, and to agree both that they are teachers and that virtue is something teachable?

[463]   MENO: No, by Zeus, Socrates, for sometimes you can hear from them that it is something teachable, and sometimes that it is not.

[464]   SOCRATES: Should we affirm then that these men, about whom there is no agreement on this very thing, are teachers of this subject?

[465]   MENO: It does not seem so to me, Socrates.

[466]   SOCRATES: Well, what then? Do these Sophists, who alone proclaim it, seem to you to be teachers of virtue?

95C   [467]   MENO: Now that is something I admire most in Gorgias, Socrates, that you would never hear him promising this, but he even laughs at the others whenever he hears them promising that. But he does think that there is a need to make men speak skillfully.

[468]   SOCRATES: Then the Sophists do not seem to you to be teachers?

[469]   MENO: I cannot say, Socrates. For I too undergo the very thing that most people do: sometimes it seems to me they are and sometimes not.

[470]   SOCRATES: Do you know that it seems so not only to you and to the other political men, that some times they think this is teachable and other times not; but do you know that Theognis the poet, too, says these same things?

95D

[471]   MENO: In which verses?

[472]   SOCRATES: In his elegiacs, where he says:

> Drink and eat with them, and with them sit,
> And gratify them whose power is great.
> For from good men you will be taught good things.
> But if you mingle with the bad, you will simply lose
> Even the mind you have.   95E

Do you see that in these verses he speaks of virtue as being something teachable?

[473]   MENO: It does appear so.

[474]   SOCRATES: But in other verses, he changes course a bit: "And if it was able to be done," he says, "and intelligence could be put into a man,"—he says something like that— many and great fees would they bear off, those who could do this," and,

> Never would a bad man be born from a good father,
> Being persuaded by sober speech. But by teaching   96A
> You will never make the bad man good.

Do you understand that he is saying opposite things about the same things to himself again?

[475]   MENO: It appears so.

[476]   SOCRATES: Can you tell me then of any other subject whatever where these who affirm that they are teachers are not only not acknowledged by others to be teachers but are not even recognized as understanding it themselves, being regarded instead as worthless in the very subject in   96B which they declare themselves to be teachers—while, on the other hand, those who are acknowledged gentlemen sometimes declare it to be teachable and, at other times, not? Could you declare that people who are so confused by any subject are, in any authoritative sense, teachers of it?

[477]   MENO: By Zeus, I certainly could not.

[478]   SOCRATES: Then if neither the Sophists nor those who are themselves gentlemen are teachers of the subject, is it clear that there could not be any other teachers of it?

[479]   MENO: It does not seem so to me.

[480]   SOCRATES: And if there are no teachers, there are no   96C learners?

[481]   MENO: It seems to me to be as you say.

[482]   SOCRATES: And have we agreed that this subject, of which there were neither teachers nor learners, is not teachable?

[483]   MENO: We have agreed.

[484]   SOCRATES: Then of virtue there appear to be no teachers anywhere?

[485]   MENO: That is so.

[486]   SOCRATES: And if no teachers, then no learners?

[487]   MENO: It appears not.

[488]   SOCRATES: Therefore virtue could not be something teachable?

96D   [489]   MENO: It's not likely, if we were looking at it correctly. So that I really wonder, Socrates, whether perhaps there are no good men, or what could be the way of generation for good men to come to be?

[490]   SOCRATES: There is a danger, Meno, that I and you are both sort of worthless men, and that Gorgias has not sufficiently educated you, nor Prodicus me. So that, above all, we should apply our minds to our very selves, and
96E   seek whoever will make us better in some one particular way: and I say this, first focusing my gaze on the search just made, how ridiculously it has escaped us that it is not only when knowledge is directing that human beings act rightly and well in their affairs, and perhaps that is why knowing in what sort of way men become good has also escaped us.

[491]   MENO: How do you mean this, Socrates?

[492]   SOCRATES: In this way: that good men are required to be
97A   beneficent; we have agreed rightly that this could not be otherwise. Is that not so?

[493]   MENO: Yes.

[494]   SOCRATES: And that they will be beneficent whenever they direct our affairs rightly, I suppose we were right in agreeing to this too?

[495]   MENO: Yes.

[496]   SOCRATES: But that it is not possible to direct rightly, if

one is not prudent, in this we are like those who have not rightly agreed.

[497]   MENO: How, indeed, do you mean "rightly"?

[498]   SOCRATES: I'll tell you. If someone who knows the road to Larissa, or any other place you want, went there and directed others, would he not direct them rightly and well?

[499]   MENO: Certainly.

[500]   SOCRATES: And what if someone is right in his opinion about what the road is, but has not gone there, nor knows the road, would he not also direct them rightly?   **97B**

[501]   MENO: Certainly.

[502]   SOCRATES: And just as long as he would have right opinion about those things of which another has knowledge, himself supposing what is the truth, but not prudently knowing it, he will be no worse a guide than he who prudently knows it.

[503]   MENO: No worse, I agree.

[504]   SOCRATES: True opinion, therefore, is no worse a guide to right action than prudence. And this is what just now we were leaving aside in our examination about what sort of thing virtue might be, when we said that only prudence   **97C** directs action rightly, whereas true opinion does so too.

[505]   MENO: That is likely.

[506]   SOCRATES: Right opinion, therefore, is no less beneficial than knowledge.

[507]   MENO: To this extent, Socrates, that he who has knowledge would always hit the mark, whereas he who has right opinion would sometimes hit it, and sometimes not.

[508]   SOCRATES: How do you mean that? Would not he that always has right opinion always hit on it, just so long as his opinions were right?

[509]   MENO: Necessarily, it appears to me. So that I wonder, Socrates, this being so, that knowledge is always so much   **97D** more honored than right opinion, and why one of them is so different from the other.

[510]   SOCRATES: Do you know then why you wonder, or should I tell you?

[511]   MENO: Certainly, tell me.

[512]   SOCRATES: Because you have never applied your mind to the statues of Daedalus. But perhaps there are none among you.

[513]   MENO: With a view to what do you say this?

[514]   SOCRATES: Because if they have not been tied down, they make their escape and run away; but if they are tied down, they stay put.

97E   [515]   MENO: Well, what about it?

[516]   SOCRATES: To have acquired one of his works that has been let loose is not worth very much, like acquiring a runaway slave, for he does not stay put; but one that is tied down is worth a great deal. For his works are very beautiful. With a view to what, then, do I say this? With a view to true opinions. For true opinions too, for as long a time as they should stay put, are a fine thing and accomplish all kinds of good things. Yet much of the time they are not willing to stay put, but run away out of the human soul; so that they are not worth much until someone should bind them with causes by reasoning. And this, my comrade Meno, is recollection, as we agreed before. And whenever they have been bound, first they become knowledge and then steadfast. And this is why knowledge is worth more than right opinion, and, by its binding, knowledge differs from and excels right opinion.

98A

[517]   MENO: By Zeus, Socrates, it is like something of this sort.

[518]   SOCRATES: And yet, I too speak, not as one who knows, but as one who makes images and conjectures. But I certainly do not think I am making images or guessing this, that right opinion and knowledge are different things. But if there is anything I could affirm that I know, and there are few I could affirm—one of those, at any rate, which I could set down that I know is this.

98B

[519]   MENO: And you are right, Socrates, in saying this.

[520]   SOCRATES: What then? Is the following not rightly said, that true opinion directing the work of each action brings it to completion no worse than knowledge?

[521]   MENO: In this, too, you seem to me to speak the truth.

[522]   SOCRATES: Then right opinion will be no worse, nor less

beneficial, in actions than knowledge, nor the man having right opinion than the one having knowledge. **98C**

[523] MENO: That is so.

[524] SOCRATES: And we did agree that the good man is beneficent.

[525] MENO: Yes.

[526] SOCRATES: Now then, since not only through knowledge can men be good and beneficial to their cities, if they would, but also through right opinion; and neither of these two is natural to human beings, neither knowledge nor true opinion, nor are they acquired—or does it seem **98D** to you that either of them is by nature?

[527] MENO: Not to me.

[528] SOCRATES: Then since they are not by nature, neither could the good men be such by nature.

[529] MENO: Surely not.

[530] SOCRATES: Since they are not such by nature, we looked next into whether it is something teachable.

[531] MENO: Yes.

[532] SOCRATES: Then did it not seem to be teachable, if virtue is prudence?

[533] MENO: Yes.

[534] SOCRATES: And if it should be something teachable, it would be prudence?

[535] MENO: Certainly.

[536] SOCRATES: And if there should be teachers, it would be teachable, but if there are not, not teachable? **98E**

[537] MENO: Quite so.

[538] SOCRATES: But surely we have agreed that there are no teachers of it?

[539] MENO: That is so.

[540] SOCRATES: We have agreed, therefore, that it is neither teachable nor prudence?

[541] MENO: Certainly.

[542] SOCRATES: But surely we agree that it is a good thing?

[543]   MENO: Yes.

[544]   SOCRATES: And what directs rightly is beneficial and good?

[545]   MENO: Certainly.

99A

[546]   SOCRATES: And these two things only direct rightly: true opinion and knowledge, which the human being who directs rightly has. For things which turn out rightly from some sort of chance do not come about through human direction. But those things, through which a human being is a director to what is right, are these two, true opinion and knowledge.

[547]   MENO: This is the way it seems to me.

[548]   SOCRATES: Then since it is not something teachable, virtue indeed does not come into being consequent to knowledge?

[549]   MENO: It appears not.

99B

[550]   SOCRATES: Therefore of two things which are good and beneficial, one of them has been let off, and in political action it could not be knowledge that directs.

[551]   MENO: It seems not, to me.

[552]   SOCRATES: It is not, therefore, by any wisdom or by being wise that such men direct their cities, Themistocles and those like him and those about whom Anytus here was just speaking. And, indeed, this is why they are unable to make others such as they are themselves, inasmuch as it is not through knowledge that they are the kind of men they are.

[553]   MENO: It is likely to be just as you say, Socrates.

[554]   SOCRATES: Then if not by knowledge, what remains, indeed, comes to be by good judgment based on opinion, which is what political men use when they straighten out their cities. They are not in a different situation with respect to prudent understanding than soothsayers or inspired diviners. For these, too, when they are inspired, do say true things, very many of them, but they do not know what they say.

99C

[555]   MENO: It probably is that way.

[556]   SOCRATES: Then, Meno, do these men deserve to be called

divine who, having no intelligence, set straight many great matters in the things that they do and say?

[557] MENO: Certainly.

[558] SOCRATES: We could, therefore, rightly call divine those about whom we were just now speaking, soothsayers and diviners and all poetic people; and the political people are not least of those whom we might affirm to be divine and divinely inspired, being inspired and possessed by the god, whenever by their speaking they set straight many great affairs, without knowing those things about which they speak. 99D

[559] MENO: Certainly.

[560] SOCRATES: And women too, surely, Meno, call good men divine. And the Laconians, whenever they praise any good man, say, "This man's divine."

[561] MENO: And it appears, Socrates, that they speak rightly. And yet, perhaps Anytus here is annoyed with you for speaking this way. 99E

[562] SOCRATES: That doesn't matter to me. We will, Meno, indeed converse with him again. But now, if we in this whole account both searched rightly and were speaking rightly, virtue would be neither by nature, nor something teachable, but has come by divine dispensation without intelligence in those to whom it might come, unless there should be that sort of man among the political men who could also make someone else politic. And if there should be one, he could almost be said to be among the living what Homer said Tiresias was among the dead, saying about him that "he alone of those in Hades has his wits about him, but the others flit about as shadows." The same would hold here too, such a man would be as a true thing alongside shadows, in regard to virtue. 100A

[563] MENO: You have spoken most beautifully, it seems to me, Socrates. 100B

[564] SOCRATES: Then from this reasoning, Meno, virtue appears to have come to us by divine dispensation, for those to whom it may come. But we shall know what is clear about it when, before we seek whatever way virtue comes to human beings, we will first undertake to seek what virtue, itself in itself, is. Now it's time for me to go, but you persuade your guest-friend Anytus here too

100C

about those very same things that you yourself have been persuaded, so that he may be more gentle: for if you do persuade him, you will also confer upon the Athenians a benefit.

NOTES

The subtitle (*Or, About Virtue: Testing*) and the list of characters (Meno, Socrates, Meno's [Slave] Boy, Anytus) for this dialogue may be later editorial additions to Plato's manuscript. See Alfred Mollin and Robert Williamson, *An Introduction to Ancient Greek* (3d ed.; Lanham, Maryland: University Press of America, 1997), p. 309. See, also, Diogenes Laertius, *Lives of Eminent Philosophers*, III, 59-60.

The dramatic action of the dialogue is said to take place a few years before the prosecution, conviction, and execution of Socrates (in 399 BCE). See Mollin and Williamson, *An Introduction to Ancient Greek*, p. 377. See, also, the notes for Speeches 156 (78D), 412 (90A) and 412 (90B).

Plato was born in about 429 and died in 347 BCE. His parents were Athenians of distinguished lineage.

The endnotes which follow are keyed to Speech numbers accompanied by Stephanus numbers, as are the cross-references among the endnotes.

MENO AND SOCRATES

1 (70A). "Virtue" translates *aretê*. *Aretê* is a very broad word in classical Greek. For example, Thucydides, in his *History of the Peloponnesian War*, writes of "the virtue of the soil" of certain parts of Greece. (I, ii, 4) Plato, early in the extensive discussion of human virtue in his *Republic*, writes of the virtue of a dog (the first mention of "virtue" in that dialogue), of a horse, and of a pruning-knife. (335B, 352D-353E, especially 353B) Whenever anything, natural being or artifact, excels at the work it is constituted by nature or by art to do, it is said to possess its proper virtue, its specific excellence. The virtue of a living body, or of a body part is health, for example, of an eye, to see well. The more complicated that living beings are, the more complicated is likely to be the inquiry into their virtues and into what might be their commanding, or fundamental, virtue. See Speech 11 (72A) of this dialogue. The word *aretê* is said to be derived from the name of the god of war, *Arês*, or, more fittingly, from the verb *arariskein*, "to fit together", or "to be fitting". See, on the relation between the beautiful and the virtuous, the notes for Speeches 113 (77B) and 404 (89C).

"Something teachable" translates *didakton*, a neuter verbal adjective which can also mean "something taught". If the feminine rather than the neuter form had been used, the word "virtue" [*aretê*] would have been its unambiguous antecedent, and there would have been no need for the word "something". The same neuter forms are used in this speech of Meno's for the words referring to practice and learning. See, on Meno as "acquisitive", the notes for Speeches 113 (77B) and 469 (95C). See, also, the note for Speech 526 (98D).

"Something... from practice" translates *askêton*, from the verb *askein*. Practice here is used in the sense of practicing the piano, exercising, training, discipline. It is the word from which the English word "ascetic" is derived. (The modern English word has shifted the emphasis to what is renounced, away from the discipline and its goal for the sake of which ordinary pleasures and pastimes are given up.) The repetitive applications of practice are apt to form habits. But there is an ambiguity here: good practice forms good habits, bad practice forms bad habits. That there are only a few explicit references to habit in this dialogue should not be taken as an index of its importance. See Speeches 2 (70B), 70 (75A), 106 (76D), 197 (82A), and especially 356 (86D). See, also, the note for Speech 355 (86C-D). See, as well, the notes for Speeches 274 (83E-84A) and 282 (84B-C).

2 (70A). "*Thessaly*, a district of northern Greece. ... [M]ountain barriers impede communication by land with neighboring areas... Owing to the extent of its plains, Thessaly was richer in grain, horses, and cattle than other parts of Greece... A few baronial families gradually became supreme ... in the sixth century [BCE]. The rivalries of aristocratical houses and the [Persian sympathies] of the Aleuadae soon caused a decline, which was intensified during the fifth century by social unrest, as the urbanization of this backward district gradually broke down baronial domination." *The Oxford Classical Dictionary* (1961), p. 900. (Most of the dates in these endnotes are taken from *The Oxford Classical Dictionary*.)

See the note for Speech 2 (70B).

2 (70B). "Wisdom" translates *sophia*, sometimes in the sense of theoretical wisdom, the deepest and most comprehensive understanding. It usually suggests the precision of expertise, a knowledge that is based on clear insight into the causes and reasons that constitute the evidence for that knowledge. The word *philosophia*, "philosophy" (*philo*—"love of" *sophia*—"wisdom") suggests that *sophia* is the goal sought by philosophers. It is frequently connected to and distinguished from *phronêsis*, "practical wisdom". See the notes for Speeches 26 (73A), 382 (88B), and 396-399 (89A). See, on the Sophists, the note for Speech 322 (85B).

"Responsible" translates *aitios*. See the note for Speech 516 (98A).

Gorgias, of Leontini (c. 483-376 BCE), was one of the most prominent of those men called Sophists. He is a major character in the Platonic dialogue named after him. See Aristotle, *Politics* 1260a27, 1275b75; Aristotle, *Rhetoric*, 1414b31, 1416a1, 1418a33, 1419b3. See, also, Speech 467 (95C) and the note for Speech 11 (72A). See, as well, the notes for Speeches 322 (85B), 426 (92A), and 469 (95C).

The city referred to is Larissa, the chief city of Thessaly. It lies about one hundred and forty miles from Athens, in a northerly direction. (The sea voyage from Athens to Larissa could require more than two hundred miles.) See Speeches 498-503 (96A-B). See, also, Aristotle, *Politics* 1275b27. "[Larissa] was the first Thessalian city to strike coins, and its earliest issues, struck on the Persian standard, reflect both the [Persian sympathies] of the Aleuadae and their influence over the Larisseans." *The Oxford Classical Dictionary*, p. 480. See the note for Speech 170 (79A). The Aleuadae were the ruling family in Thessaly. See the notes for Speeches 2 (70A), 104 (76E) and 116 (77C). See, on Aristippus, the note for Speech 156 (78D). See, on the general reputation of Thessalians with respect to wisdom, Plato, *Crito* 53D-54A.

2 (71A). Compare Speech 437 (92E). Compare, also, Speech 469 (95C).

2 (71B). "Cognizance" translates *gignōskein*. It is the kind of knowing one gets through perception, acquaintance, or recognition. Consider the use of words with the same root, *gnō-*, in the first chapter of Aristotle's *Physics*. See Jacob Klein, *A Commentary on Plato's Meno* (Chapel Hill: University of North Carolina Press, 1965), pp. 42, 84-85. See, also, the note for Speech 204 (82D). See, as well, the note for Speech 162 (78E).

"At all" translates *to parapan*, which can also mean "altogether". The term is used three times by Socrates in Speech 2 (71A-B). See, on Socrates' first speech in the *Meno*, George Anastaplo, *On Trial: From Adam & Eve to O.J. Simpson* (Lanham, Maryland: Lexington Books, forthcoming), Chap. 6-A (adapted from *The Great Ideas Today* [Encyclopedia Britannica], vol. 1997, pp. 4-9 [1997]). See, on nature as a guide for human action, Anastaplo, *But Not Philosophy: Seven Introductions to Non-Western Thought* (Lanham, Maryland: Lexington Books, 2002), pp. 303-43, 387 (index). See, also, the notes for Speeches 2 (71B), 474 (95E-96A) and 526 (98D).

8 (71C-D). "Remembering", *mnêsis*, is distinguished from "reminding", or "recollecting", *anamnesis*. The Greek word *ana* is the preposition "up" or "upwards"; as a prefix it can mean "up", or "back", or "again", like the English prefix "re-". Prefixing *ana-* to the ordinary word for memory or remembering suggests setting out to recall, or to bring something back up to memory. "Remind me" translates *anamnêson ... me*. See the note for Speech 194 (81C).

10 (71D). The phrase translated as "fortunate falsehood" could also mean "so that I have been deceived by a most fortunate deception".

The first of the dozen oaths in the dialogue is in this speech. A listing of these oaths may be found in Appendix A of this volume.

11 (71E). The minimal meaning of "freeman" is someone who is not owned by another, as a slave is. A further meaning is suggested by Socrates in Speech 356 (86D). See, also, the note for that Speech. See, as well, the note for Speech 26 (73A).

11 (72A). "Difficulty" translates *aporia*. See the note for Speech 162 (78E).

"Task" translates *ergon*. *Ergon* can also be translated, in different contexts, as "function", "work" or "deed". Compare Plato, *Republic* 335D, 352D-353E.

"Good" translates *agathos* (as in Speech 32 [73B]). Its opposite, "bad" or "evil", *kakos* is used here. The opposite to the word translated "virtue", *aretê* (see the note for Speech 1 [70A]), is derived from *kakos*, namely, *kakia*, translated as "vice". Both *kakos* and *kakia* are used in Speech 11 (71E-72A).

Aristotle approves of Meno's (and Gorgias') way of enumerating the virtues. See his *Politics* 1259b21-1260b7, especially 1260a25-28. Compare Plato, *Theaetetus* 146C sq.

Seth Benardete has suggested that Meno said here that "virtue consists in doing one's job well." *The Argument of the Action: Essays on Greek Poetry and Philosophy* (Chicago: University of Chicago Press, 2000), p. 302. See, also, the note for Speech 24 (73A). See, as well, Plato, *Republic* 433 sq.

12 (72A). "Seeking" translates *zêtôn*, which is a form of the verb *zêtein*, meaning "to seek", "to seach for", or "to inquire". Its fuller meaning is explored throughout this dialogue. See Speeches 41 (73D), 42 (73D), 52 (74A), 53 (74A), 174 (79D), 176 (79D), 184 (80D), 185 (80D) (two times), 186 (80E) (four times), 194 (81E), 352 (86B-C), 354 (86C), 356 (86D), 420 (90E), 490 (96D-E), 562 (99E), 564 (100B). See, especially, the notes for Speeches 66 (74E) and 194 (81E).

12 (72B). "Very being" translates *ousia*, a word probably derived from the feminine participle *ousa*, of the verb *einai*, "to be", that without which a thing would cease to be what it is. Our word "essence" would be an adequate translation for anyone who remembers that the Latin *essentia* is derived from the Latin verb *esse*, "to be".

14 (72C). The final question in this speech could also be translated, "You could, surely, have something to say to me?"

16 (72C). "Form" translates *eidos*, which is often translated as "idea". *Eidos* is also sometimes translated as "class", as "character", and as "pattern". The elementary meaning of the word is "looks", that by which someone or something is recognized as being who or what he, she, or it is. It is connected to the verb *eidenai*, "to know", the original meaning of which is "to have seen". The sense of the word is that one knows what one has seen. Consider the familiar saying, "Seeing is believing." See the note for Speech 81 (75C).

Immanuel Kant argued, "Even if sight is no more indispensable than hearing, it is still the noblest of the senses. For it is furthest removed from the sense of touch, the most limited condition of perception: it not only has the widest sphere of perception in terms of space, but it is also the sense in which we are least aware of the organs being affected (since otherwise it would not be merely sight). So sight comes closest to a *pure intuition* (an immediate representation of the given object, with no admixture of sensation noticeable in it)." *Anthropology from a Pragmatic Point of View*, Mary J. Gregor, trans. (The Hague: Martinus Nijhoff, 1974), § 19, p. 35.

An important question for Plato and Aristotle is how the elementary notion of "sensible looks" becomes transmuted into the idea of "intelligible *(noetic)* looks". It has something to do with the fact that that by virtue of which a being is what it is, is also that by virtue of which it belongs to a class. When we say, "This is a dog," we also mean, "This belongs to the class of dogs." What gives a being its character has the attribute of a class character.

"That to which the question 'What is?' points is the *eidos* of a thing, the shape or form or character or 'idea' of a thing. It is no accident that the term *eidos* signifies primarily that which is visible to all without any particular effort or that which one might call the 'surface' of the things." Leo Strauss, *Natural Right and History* (Chicago: University of Chicago Press, 1953), p. 123. See, also, *ibid.*, pp. 120f; Plato, *Phaedo* 98 sq.

24 (73A). "Manage" translates *dioikein*, which means literally "to manage a household *(oikia)* thoroughly" *(dia-)*. It is metaphorically extended to the managing and governing of larger institutions like cities. Meno, in defining the virtue of a woman, had used the verb *oikein*, "manage a household", but for the virtue of a man, he had used *prattein*, "to carry on the affairs of". Socrates does not repeat here what Meno *was saying*; rather, he seems, by the implications of his language, deliberately to be blurring the differences in what had been asserted by Meno in Speech 11 (71E). See the note for Speech 11 (72A). See, also, the note for Speech 153 (78C).

26 (73A). *Sôphrosunê* has variously been translated as "moderation", "temperance", "soundness of mind", "self-control", "discretion", "sobriety", and "modesty". The *sô-* part of the word means "saving", "preserving", or "soundness of"; the *phro* is the *phron* of the word *phronêsis*. (See on prudence and practical wisdom, the notes for Speeches 2 [70B], 382 [88B], and 396-399 [89A]). This word, with its two parts together, suggests soundness of practical intelligence or practical thoughtfulness. It seems to be the virtue preparatory to, and culminating in, practical wisdom. See Plato, *Cratylus* 411E-412A; Plato, *Republic* 431C-D, 432A.

In the *Republic*, where moderation is described and defined, Plato has Socrates speak of human beings as masters of, or in control of, themselves. *Republic* 430D-432B. What the phrase wants to say, and is generally understood to say, is, according to Socrates, that in every human being the soul has a better and a worse part: self-mastery or self-control, as a term of praise, means the control of an inferior part by the part that is by nature superior. On an ordinary level that means ruling one's desires, pleasures and pains with respect to food, drink and sexual gratification. *Republic* 389D-E. Moderation, when it rises above mere self-control, becomes, however rarely, "adhering to those simple and measured desires, pleasures and pains which are both accompanied by intelligence and guided by the reasoning of right opinion." *Republic* 431C. See the note for Speech 356 (86D).

Moderation, unlike two of the other cardinal virtues, courage and wisdom, which are each virtues of some special part of the soul (namely, spiritedness and reason), is found in an order of relations extending over and between all the different parts of the soul. (Wisdom may be either *sophia* or *phronêsis*. The fourth cardinal virtue is justice. See the note for Speeches

45-46 [73D-E] and 51 [74A].) On the highest level, moderation as a goal is defined as that beautiful order, "concord and harmony of the naturally inferior and superior as to which of them ought to rule both in the city and in each individual." *Republic*, 432A-B. This disposition or state of the soul is a necessary precondition for practical wisdom, *phronêsis*, which, when it is added to moderation in this fullest sense, makes for what Aristotle calls (in the final chapter of Book VI of the *Nicomachean Ethics*) governing, or authoritative, virtue.

Moderation is the principal topic of Plato's *Charmides*. Although none of the definitions offered there is shown to be successful standing alone, there is never an attempt to pull them all together. Whether moderation in the highest sense is attainable for human beings is touched on in Plato's *Phaedrus* 246E sq., especially 247E-248B.

45-46 (73D-E). The sense in which justice might be thought to be virtue is examined in Aristotle *Nicomachean Ethics*, V, i. Both Plato (especially in his *Republic* and in his *Gorgias*) and Aristotle (in Book V of his *Nicomachean Ethics* and Book III of his *Politics*) speak of justice both as an order between the parts of the souls of individuals and as an order of different kinds of persons within the whole of political society, the two orders being mutually interdependent. It becomes difficult to distinguish part of what is said about justice within individual souls from what is said about moderation. See the notes for Speeches 26 (73A) and 170 (79A).

51 (74A). See, on the cardinal virtues (three of which are listed here [justice is omitted]), the note for Speech 26 (73A). See, on those virtues and on the virtue of magnificence, Aristotle, *Nicomachean Ethics*, Books III-V.

60 (74C). See, on color, the notes for Speeches 78 (75B-C) and 81 (75C).

66 (74E). Jacob Klein speaks of Socrates' "painstakingly precise" manner of "seeking, and finding" in this part of the dialogue. *A Commentary on Plato's Meno*, p. 57. The dialogue is not clear about whether, in its discussion of "round" and "straight", it is referring to surfaces or lines; both are encompassed by shape or figure. In Speech 64 (74D) Socrates refers to the fact that we use one word, "shape", to refer to figures that are sensibly and manifestly different, even in some respects opposite to one another. Furthermore, these words might refer not to sensible manifestations, lines, and surfaces, but rather to the forms or ideas of shape, of roundness, and of straightness. In Speech 53 (74A-B), Meno speaks of his inability to understand Socrates' way of seeking. (Compare the note for Speech 357 [87C].) Socrates seems to be providing here an exercise which, through ordinary language, attempts to show Meno that he has been dealing with forms and ideas all his speaking life. The precision referred to by Klein lies in the spelling out of general ideas, and how they relate to the ideas and things encompassed by them. Classes that are mutually exclusive may share intelligible characteristics that make for their being subsumed under one and the same more general class.

In Speeches 64-65 (74D-E) Socrates and Meno agree that something which is round is no more a shape or figure than something which is straight is a shape or figure. Socrates, in Speech 66 (74E), in order to illustrate how classes or their ideas which are opposite to one another have relations to one another that are different from the relations they both have to the general idea under which they are subsumed, tries out the argument of Speech 64 (74D-E) with ideas of opposites to show that there it fails. The obvious assumption is that the round is "more" round than the straight, and that the straight is "more" straight than the round. So when Socrates asks (in Speech 66 [74E]) whether Meno would affirm that the "no more" argument of Socrates' previous speech applies—that is, "that the round is no more round than straight and the straight no more straight than round"—Meno correctly responds, "Certainly not" (Speech 67 [74E]). Consider, as illustrative of the approach here, the observation that although even numbers are not numbers "more" than odd numbers are numbers, it is not the case that even numbers are not more even than odd numbers are, nor is it the case that odd numbers are not more odd than even numbers are.

What both modern readers and ancient companions seem to find puzzling is Socrates' insistence upon precise analysis of the "perfectly obvious".

72 (75B). "Gratify" seems to mean here, to spare Meno the work of "serious practice". See also Speeches 92-93 (76C).

78 (75B-C). Jacob Klein argues that the complementarity of color and shape here suggests the complementarity of knowledge and virtue. He refers to a proportion that can be put thus:

color : shape : body :: knowledge : virtue : soul.

See *A Commentary on Plato's Meno*, pp. 59-60. That is, virtue is not identical with knowledge, but we never find virtue without finding knowledge and we never find knowledge without finding virtue: they are "coextensive". See, also, the note for Speech 356 (86E-87B). See, as well, the note for Speech 81 (75C).

81 (75C). "Know" translates *eidenai*, the original meaning of which is "to have seen". See the note for Speech 16 (72C).

"Is at a loss about it" translates a verbal form of the word discussed in the note for Speech 162 (78E).

The word translated here as "color" includes the white and the black, in the sense of visible surface. Meno's statement here has the collateral meaning: "Suppose someone should affirm that he has not seen color, or has not seen a visible surface..." Consider Speeches 60-63 (74C-D).

82 (75C). "A bent for strife" translates *eristikos*. *Eris* is the goddess *Strife*. See Homer, *Iliad*, IV, 440-45, XI, 1-14. See, also, the notes for Speeches 82 (75D) and 194 (81D).

82 (75C-D). "More dialectical" translates *dialektikôteron*; the infinitive form *dialegesthai* is translated by "to have a discussion", "to have a conversation", "to converse". The related word *dialectic* from the Greek *dialektikê* is referred to as a "study" (*mathêma*) and as a "pursuit" (*methodos*—a hunting word) in Plato's *Republic* 534E, 533C. The English "dialogue" is from the related Greek word *dialogos*. The *lek-, leg-*, and *log-* in these words are derived from the infinitive *legein* and its noun *logos*. *Legein* is usually translated by "say", or by "mean" (see Speech 114 [77B]); but it can also mean "to gather", "to select", "to count." It may be seen in the English words "collect", "elect", and "select". It is, therefore, not mere talking, but rather thoughtful, meaningful, selected speaking. The infinitive *dialegein* means "to divide", "to distinguish", or "to pick" and "to sort out".

The word *dia*, connected to the word for "two" (*duo*), in compositions like this, signifies connections between two or more separated things. For example, the word *bainein* means "to walk", the word *diabainein* means "to cross a bridge". A dialectical conversation attempts to bridge the gaps of understanding between participants.

In Plato's *Republic* (511B), Socrates speaks of "the power of dialectic" (where *dialegesthai* pulls together both meanings: "to converse" and "to sort out"), that power by which "rational discourse" (*logos*) engages in that highest form of inquiry which ascends toward first principles. Dialectic is there contrasted with the hypothetical method of mathematics and its kindred arts, which cannot rise to first principles, because of its inability to rise above its assumptions. See Speech 356 (86D-87C) and the note for Speech 356 (86E).

See, on "Dialectic and Recollection in Plato's *Meno*," Laurence Berns, *Politics, Nature, and Piety* (Lanham, Maryland: Lexington Books, forthcoming); Berns, "Socratic and Non-Socratic Philosophy," *Review of Metaphysics*, vol. 28, p. 85 (1974).

82 (75D). Aristotle wrote a book on false, or sophistical, refutations, in which "contentious arguments" are defined as arguments "which reason or seem to reason from opinions which appear to be, but are not really, generally accepted." *Sophistical Refutations*, II, 165b8-9. See, also, the first chapter of Aristotle's *Topics*.

82 (75E). Prodicus of Ceos was a Sophist known for his great interest in the exact meanings of words. See, e.g., Plato, *Protagoras* 337A, 340C-341C, 358A-E.

"Fancy" translates *poikilon*, which also means "multi-colored".

86 (76A). Here, as Klein puts it, "Socrates, following Meno, has abandoned the colloquial meaning of *schêma* ["shape", "figure"] altogether. In the definition [Socrates] has just given, the word does not mean 'closed surface of a visible thing' but a geometrical entity, 'figure', as defined [later], for example, in Euclid: 'Figure is that which is contained by any boundary or boundaries,' where 'boundary', in turn, is defined as the limit (*peras*) of something. *Schêma* in Socrates' second definition is a 'technical' word signifying a 'bounded surface area'..." *A Commentary on Plato's Meno*, p. 65 (citing Euclid,

Elements I, Def. 14, Def. 13). Klein notes that *peras* ("limit") is not defined in Euclid. *Ibid.*, p. 65 n. 31. See, also, *ibid.*, pp. 63-67.

Meno does not ask here, as he in effect had about color, "What is a solid?" Is this partly because Socrates had just taken the rhetorical precaution of asking in advance whether there was something that Meno called a solid?

88 (76A). "Outrageous" translates a variant of the now-fashionable word *hubris*, which, according to context, can also mean "wanton violence", "insolence", "bullying", "running riot", "maliciousness", "insulting", "overbearing", and "licentious". A shameless and boastful exulting seems to accompany the insulting activities of the hubristic man or woman. There was at Athens a "law of hubris" to punish serious injuries resulting from malicious assault. See Henry George Liddell and Robert Scott, *A Greek-English Lexicon* (*hubris*).

90 (76B). "Handsome" translates *kalos*, the masculine form for the adjective "beautiful". See the notes for Speeches 113 (77B) and 404 (89C).

92-93 (76C). See the note for Speech 72 (75B).

96 (76C). Empedocles of Acragas in Sicily (c. 493-c. 433 BCE) is traditionally associated with the Pythagoreans. He presented his corporealist philosophy of nature in poetic form. All things are governed by the "mingling [Love] and separation [Strife]" of elemental Fire, Water, Earth and Air. The bodily senses are "the way" (*poros*) to "understanding" (*noêsai*). See Hermann Diels, *Fragmente der Vorsokratiker*, fragments 17 and 3, I, pp. 315-18, 310-11. See, also Richard S. Bluck, *Plato's Meno* (Cambridge: Harvard University Press, 1961) pp. 251-52; John Burnet, *Early Greek Philosophy* (London and Edinburgh: Adam and Charles Black, 1892), chap. V; Kathleen Freeman, *Ancilla to the Presocratic Philosophers* (Cambridge: Harvard University Press, 1957), pp. 51-69.

98-104 (76C-D). See, on Empedocles' effluences, Bluck, *Plato's Meno*, pp. 252-53.

104 (76D). Pindar (518-438 BCE), the great lyric poet of Boeotia, was born in Cynoscephalae, near Thebes. A large number of his epinician (victory-celebrating) odes and fragments survive. His first commission for an epinician ode came from the powerful Aleuadae family of Thessaly. See *The Odes of Pindar* (Loeb Classical Library, 1946), p. ix. See, also, the note for Speech 2 (70B).

See, on the sources of the words here attributed to Pindar, Klein, *A Commentary on Plato's Meno*, pp. 68-70; Bluck, *Plato's Meno*, pp. 251-52. Bluck writes, about Socrates' reference to Pindar here, "In the present passage they add to the general air of mock-profundity." *Ibid.*, p. 251.

108 (76E). "Tragical", that is, high-flown and deep-sounding.

110 (76E). The dialogue, until Speech 354 (86C), might be considered to be an examination of why Socrates thinks "the other one" (which other?) is the better answer. Consider Klein, *A Commentary on Plato's Meno*, pp. 65f; Plato, *Republic* 619B-D.

110-111 (76E-77A). The *Mysteries* alluded to are probably the Lesser Mysteries celebrated at Eleusis, a place near Athens. See Bluck, *Plato's Meno*, p. 254. They were in honor of Demeter and Persephone, attracting the pious (as well as the curious?) from all of Greece. See *The Oxford Classical Dictionary*, pp. 313, 593-94. See, on Persephone, the note for Speech 194 (81B-C). See, also, the note for Speech 562 (100A).

112 (77A). There is a strange proliferation of strong "buts" in this speech.

113 (77B). The word for "beautiful", *kalôs*, can be translated "noble" (in the sense of "beyond the call of duty") in ethical and political contexts. But "noble", in the sense of ethical beauty, of beauty of character, or of beauty of actions should be distinguished from "noble" in the sense of distinguished birth, for which there is another word in Greek (*gennaion*). See the notes for Speeches 404 (89C) and 494 (97A).

The poet referred to here may be Simonides of Ceos (c. 556-468 BCE).

In the otherwise unknown line of poetry that Meno quotes, the term "to be capable" (*dunasthai*) is usually supplemented by an infinitive specifying what the capability refers to. Supplements are frequently inferred according to context. Here it might be "capable of recognizing (or understanding) beautiful things." Meno immediately interprets it as "capable of acquiring". *Dunasthai*, without supplement and taken absolutely, could mean "to dominate", "to be a master over", or "to be proficient in". The poet's quotation, left to itself, is open to all of these interpretations. See, on Meno as *acquisitive*, the notes for Speeches 1 (70A) and 469 (95C). See, also, Robert Sternfeld and Harold Zyskind, *Plato's Meno: A Philosophy of Man as Acquisitive* (Carbondale: Southern Illinois University Press, 1978); Book Review, *Review of Metaphysics*, vol. 32, p. 773 (1979) (at p. 775, 1.34, "It is not true" should read, "But is it not true"). See, as well, the note for Speech 526 (98D).

Jonathan Edwards, at the outset of his 1765 essay "The Nature of True Virtue", brings together in this way the "beautiful" and the "virtuous": "Whatever controversies and variety of opinions there are about the nature of virtue, yet all (excepting some skeptics who deny any real difference between virtue and vice) mean by it something *beautiful*, or rather some kind of *beauty* or excellency. 'Tis not *all* beauty that is called virtue; for instance, not the beauty of a building, of a flower, or of the rainbow: but some beauty belonging to beings that have *perception* and *will*. 'Tis not all beauty of *mankind* that is called virtue; for instance, not the external beauty of the countenance, or shape, gracefulness of motion, or harmony of voice: but it is a beauty that has its original seat in the mind. But yet perhaps not *everything* that may be called a beauty of mind is properly called virtue. There is a beauty of understanding and speculation. There is something in the ideas and conceptions of great philosophers and statesmen that may be called beautiful, which is a different thing from what is most commonly meant by virtue. But virtue is the beauty of those qualities and acts of the mind that are of a *moral* nature, i.e. such as are attended with dessert or worthiness of *praise* or *blame*. Things of this sort, it is generally agreed, so far as I know, are not anything belonging merely to speculation; but to the *disposition* and *will*, or (to use a general word, I suppose commonly well understood) to the 'heart'. Therefore I suppose, I shall not depart from the common opinion when I say that virtue is the beauty of the qualities and exercises of the heart, or those actions which proceed from them. So that when it is inquired, what is the nature of true *virtue*? this is the same as to inquire, what that is which renders any habit, disposition, or exercise of the heart truly *beautiful*?" *A Jonathan Edwards Reader*, John E. Smith, Harry S. Stout, and Kenneth P. Minkema, eds. (New Haven: Yale University Press, 1995), p. 244. See the note for Speech 113 (77B).

Consider, also, an observation recorded in Chapter 40 of Jane Austen's *Pride and Prejudice*: "There certainly was some great mismanagement in the education of those two young men. One has got all the goodness, and the other all the appearance of goodness." Do we not yearn for a reliable correspondence among the Good, the True, and the Beautiful? See the note for Speech 138-140 (78A). See, also, the note for Speech 404 (89C).

114 (77B). "Mean" translates *legein*. See the notes for Speeches 82 (75C-D) and 186-187 (80E-81A).

116 (77C). "My very good man" translates *ôriste*, which is a contracted form of the vocative *ô ariste* (Speech 176 [79D]), which could also be translated "best of men". There is an echo here of the Thessalian aristocracy with whom Meno is associated. See the notes for Speeches 2 (70A) and 2 (70B). See, also, the note for Speech 156 (78D).

124 (77C). This speech could perhaps be more accurately translated as, "What do you mean by 'desiring'? That it should become his?"

131 (77E). "Probably do" translates *kinduneuousin*, which is connected to the word for "danger". It has a secondary meaning of "are in danger of".

136 (78A). The word for "ill-fated", *kakodaimôn*, also means "unhappy" or "wretched". The word literally means "being possessed (or attended) by an evil spirit (or deity)". Consider also the notes for Speeches 386 (88C) and 396-399 (89A).

138-140 (78A). Consider, on "wishing", Aristotle, *Nicomachean Ethics* 1111b19-29. The word translated as "to desire" *epithymein*, is strong, literally "to set one's heart (*thymos*) on (*epi*)". "Wishing", *boulesthai*, is more general: one wishes for what one desires, but one can also wish for something which one regards as impossible and hence which one cannot truly set one's heart on. See Leo Strauss, "Plato's Political Philosophy: The *Meno*" Course Transcript (The University of Chicago, Spring 1966), Lecture 6, p. 3. (The Leo Strauss course transcripts, which are being processed in a program financed by the Relm Foundation, should become available in electronic form.)

Consider the implications of the opening lines of Aristotle's *Nicomachean Ethics* and *Politics*, about everyone's inclination being toward the good. A modernist version of this hopeful insight is the observation by Jean Renoir (*The Rules of the Game*), "You see, in this world, there is one awful thing, and that is that everyone has his reasons." See the notes for Speeches 113 (77B) and 404 (89C). See, also, Speech 130 (77E).

141 (78B). See, on "I dare say", the note for Speech 131 (77E).

142 (78B). See Speech 113 (77B), and following.

148 (78B-C). Socrates, with Meno's agreement, has reduced one of Meno's speeches about virtue (Speech 113 [77B]) to (1) desiring good things and (2) having power to provide good things for oneself. Since virtue is taken to be an excellence which distinguishes one person from another (Speech 146 [78B]), and since all human beings equally partake in the desire for good things (Speech 144 [78B]), only (2) remains. Would Meno's original formulation of (1), "to desire beautiful things" (Speech 113 [77B]), have fallen prey to *this* argument?

153 (78C). Roslyn Weiss observes in her commentary on the *Meno*: "The Meno of our dialogue craves power and money. As he seeks to define virtue, his definition initially embraces the virtues of men, women, children, slaves, and old men; but when he is pressed to find a single virtue—the virtue common to all instances of virtue—his definition narrows to exclude all but the virtue associated with men, namely, that of ruling others (*M.* 73c9-d1); and in his final attempt to define virtue, he designates gold and silver, along with political honor and office, as the great goods that the man of virtue has the power to acquire (*M.* 78c7-8). Is Meno a bad man? Or [was George] Grote right to say [in 1888] that 'there is nothing in the Platonic dialogue to mark that meanness and perfidy which the Xenophontic picture indicates'?" Weiss, *Virtue in the Cave: Moral Inquiry in Plato's Meno* (New York: Oxford University Press, 2001), p. 20 (notes omitted). See the notes for Speeches 11 (72A), 156 (78D) and 194 (81A-B). See, also, the notes for Speeches 1 (70A) and 24 (73A). See, as well, the note for Speech 412 (90B).

156 (78D). "The Great King" referred to here is the Persian ruler, the most powerful and most wealthy monarch of those times. Does Meno's family owe this honor, its hereditary relation to the Great King, to its having welcomed to Thessaly the Persian invaders of Greece during the Persian War (more than a half-century before)? See Mollin and Williamson, *An Introduction to Ancient Greek*, p. 339. Xenophon, a student of Socrates, reports that Meno betrayed his Greek comrades to the Persian king and was subsequently tortured to death by him (in Persia) in about 401 BCE. *Anabasis*, II, vi, 28-29. See, also, the notes for Speeches 2 (70A) and 2 (70B).

"According to Xenophon, it was owing to Meno's relationship with Aristippus that Meno was given command of the [substantially Greek] mercenaries whom Cyrus [the Younger, the brother of the Persian king] had loaned to Aristippus and who took part, with Meno, in… the unsuccessful attempt [by Cyrus] on the Persian throne in 401 BC." Weiss, *Virtue in the Cave*, p. 18 n.4. See, on Aristippus, Speech 2 (70A-B). See, also, the note for Speech 153 (78C).

158 (78D). See, on "vice", the note for Speech 11 (72A). Vice had been introduced by Meno in that speech.

160 (78E). See the note for Speech 170 (79A).

162 (78E). "Lack of provision" translates *aporia. Aporia* can also mean "lack of means", "lack of resource", "lack of a way", as well as "perplexity", "difficulty", "impasse", "poverty". Socrates is playing with "two etymologically dissimilar but vocally similar Greek words" (Mollin and Williamson, *An Introduction to Ancient Greek*, p. 339, note 3): *poros*, "way", "passageway", (introduced in Speeches 98, 100 [76C-D]), "resource", "means", "a providing"; *ekporizein*, "to provide thoroughly", "to procure". See the notes for Speeches 179 (80A) and 184 (80C). In Plato's *Symposium*, the father of "Love", *Eros*, is said to be "Resource", *Poros*; his mother, "Poverty", *Penia*. (203B-204A) Compare "share the poverty", *sum-penomai*, in Speech 2 (71B) of the *Meno*.

170 (79A). "Change it into small coin" translates *kermatizein*. In Speech 172 (79C), "change it into pieces of small change" translates *katakermatizein …moria*. In Speech 153 (78C), Meno, in speaking of "gold" and "silver", uses diminutive forms (*-ion* at the end of a word), *chrusion* and *argurion*, which can also mean "a piece of gold" and "a piece of silver". Socrates goes along with that usage in Speech 156 (78D). In Speeches 160 (78E), 166 (79A), 170 and 172 (79A-C), Socrates picks up on Meno's use of the diminutives, using himself the word *morion* translated "piece" (plural *moria*), which could also mean "portion" or "small portion". See, on the coinage of Larissa, the note for Speech 2 (70B).

Mollin and Williamson ask about Speech 160 (78E), "Are *dikaiosunê* [justice], etc., related to *arête* [virtue] as small coin to gold?" *An Introduction to Ancient Greek*, p. 339. One might also ask, Are justice, moderation, piety, etc., related to virtue more like two, three, four and five are related to number, or more like the organs of a living body are related to the whole living body? See the notes for Speeches 26 (73A) and 45-46 (73D-E).

172 (79B). The sentence "Why then do I say this?" has been given to Meno in some texts. But John Burnet (Oxford), Alfred Croiset and Louis Robin (Budé), and our translation give it to Socrates. E. Seymer Thompson and Richard S. Bluck break up the sentence and give the first part to Meno: "Well, and what then?" and the second part to Socrates, making it the beginning of the next sentence: "I say this because when…"

174 (79D). See Speeches 82-83 (75C-D). See, also, Klein, *A Commentary on Plato's Meno*, pp. 82-87.

179 (80A). "State of perplexity" translates the verb form of the word *aporia*. See the note for Speech 162 (78E).

"Looks" translates *eidos*, rendered elsewhere in our translation as "form" (see the note for Speech 16 [72D]). There is here a rare instance of this key philosophical term used (by Meno) in its elementary non-philosophic sense.

"Drugging" translates *pharmattein* (noun form, *pharmakon*), which can mean both "to treat with drugs", or "to bewitch with potions". "Torpedo-fish" ("electric ray" or "sting ray") translates *narkê*, which can also mean "numbness". The related verb *narkân* translates into "grow numb", "making numb", and "am numb". The English words "pharmacy" and "narcotics" are derived from these words. See, on the torpedo-fish, V. Whittaker, *The Cholinergic Neuron and Its Target* (Boston: Birkhäuser, 1992), pp. 480-89 ("The Torpedo in Literature, Ancient and Modern"). See, also, the cover of this volume.

179 (80B). See the note for Speech 282 (84B-C). See, also, Anytus' Speeches 427 (92A-B) and 459 (94E-95A); Plato *Crito* 45B-C and 53B-54B.

184 (80C). "Well-provided" translates *eu-*: "well": *poros*, "provided". See the note for Speech 162 (78E).

185-186 (80D-E). See, for a challenging assessment of the teaching central to this dialogue, Alfarabi, *Philosophy of Plato and Aristotle*, Muhsin Mahdi, trans. (New York: The Free Press of Glencoe, 1962), p. 55 (II, ii, 6). See, also, the notes for Speeches 274 (83E-84A) and 282 (84B-C). See, as well, Stewart Umphrey, *Zetetic Skepticism* (Wakefield, New Hampshire: Longwood Academic, Hollowbrook Publishing, 1990), which begins with an extended analysis of these speeches.

186 (80E). See, on "strife", the notes for Speeches 82 (75C), 82 (75C-D) and 82 (75D).

186-187 (80E-81A). "Argument" translates *logos*. See the note for Speech 82 (75C-D). *Logos* can also be translated by "word", "speech", "meaning", "account" (Speech 191 [81A]), "sentence", or "(mathematical) ratio". Our word "logic" comes from another derivative, *logikos*, which means "fit for logos, fit for reasoning, fit for rational discourse".

190-191 (81A). Either Socrates pauses in mid-sentence or Meno interrupts him. Meno does seem, here, to be unable to wait.

193 (81A). Meno seems more passionately interested here than perhaps anywhere else in the dialogue. Compare Speeches 110-111 (76A-77E).

194 (81A-B). "To give an account" translates *logon didonai*. See Plato, *Phaedo* 76B. The teachers of virtue mentioned here are the teachers of the virtue of piety. Is the distinction between male and female transcended? See, e.g., the note for Speech 153 (78C). Are we being prepared here for the final argument about "divine dispensation", *theiamoira*, in Speeches 562-564 (99E-100B)?

194 (81B). "Those from whom" seem to be those who have tried to live as piously as possible.

194 (81B-C). Mollin and Williamson note, "The poem from which Socrates quotes does not survive; many scholars assign it to Pindar ... According to some accounts, Persephone, bride of Hades and Queen of Tartarus, gave birth to the god Dionysus, who was devoured by the Titans. Zeus (who may have been the father of Dionysus and Persephone alike) smote the Titans with lightning in vengeance, and from the ashes sprang man. Thus, man carries in him the stain of an ancient crime, for which he must make requital." *An Introduction to Ancient Greek*, p. 348 n.2. See, also, the notes for Speeches 110 (76E) and 562 (100A).

See on the severely limited intellectual capacity of almost everyone in Hades, Speech 562 (100A).

194 (81C). See, on recollection, the note for Speech 8 (71C-D). See, also, Joseph Cropsey, *Plato's World: Man's Place in the Cosmos* (Chicago: University of Chicago Press, 1995), pp. 54-55; Plato, *Theaetetus* 197A sq.

194 (81D). "Contentious" translates *eristikos*. See the note for Speech 82 (75C).

194 (81E). "Willing ... to seek" translates *zêtêtikous*, "ready", "able", "fit", or "disposed to seek", or "to search". The word is derived from the verb *zêtein*. See the notes for Speeches 12 (72A) and 66 (74E).

The word "zetetic" has been used by Leo Strauss to describe the fundamental characteristic of Socratic philosophizing. He often used Pascal's remark—that we know too much to be skeptics and too little to be dogmatists—to characterize Socrates' position. "[P]hilosophy in the original meaning of the term is nothing but knowledge of one's ignorance.... But one cannot know that one does not know without knowing what one does not know. What Pascal said with anti-philosophic intent about the impotence of both dogmatism and skepticism, is the only possible justification of philosophy which as such is neither dogmatic nor skeptic, and still less 'decisionist', but [rather is] zetetic (or skeptic in the original sense of the term)." Strauss, *On Tyranny*, Victor Gourevitch and Michael S. Roth, eds. (New York: The Free Press/Macmillan, 1991), p. 196. Zetetic, or open skepticism, is thus distinguished from the modern dogmatic skepticism (we know fully that we cannot know) of thinkers such as Hobbes, Descartes and Kant. See the note for Speech 426 (92A).

SOCRATES AND THE SLAVE-BOY

198 (82B). "Exhibit" translates *epideiknumi*, which is the verb from which the notion of *epideictic* rhetoric is derived. See Lane Cooper, *The Rhetoric of Aristotle* (New York: Appleton-Century Crofts, 1932), p. 17 (1.3). See, also, Larry Arnhart, *Aristotle on Political Reasoning: A Commentary on the Rhetoric* (DeKalb: Northern Illinois University Press, 1981), pp. 49-50, 77-86, 226.

204 (82B). "Know" translates *gignôskein*. See the note for Speech 2 (71B).

The language throughout the Slave-boy scene indicates that Socrates and the Boy are looking at diagrams, probably drawn on the ground or in the sand. We are expected to make diagrams for ourselves in order to follow the discussion. Detailed diagrams, prepared by us, are provided with this translation (see Appendix B of this volume). See, also, the notes for Speeches 206 (82C) and 552 (99B).

"Square" translates *tetragônon*, which literally means "four-angled". "Area" translates *chôrion*, which also means "a place", "a spot", "landed property", "geometric figure". It is connected to the verb *chôrein*, "to make room for another". See the note for Speech 356 (86E).

205 (82B). The designation *PAIS MENONOS*, "Boy of Meno", or "Meno's Boy" or "Slave-boy of Meno", could, as determined by the context, also mean "Child of Meno". The relations between Meno and the Boy may be quite complicated. See, e.g., Speech 201 (82B). See, also, the notes for Speeches 322 (85B) and 356 (86E).

206 (82C). The figure provided by us here (Figure 1) is the same as the figure just provided for Speech 204 (82B). See, for another such immediate duplication, Speeches 234 (83A) and 236 (83B). See, as well, the catalogue of less immediate duplications in Appendix B of this volume.

These figures track the steps in the geometrical development from Speech 204 (82B) through Speech 322 (85B) of the *Meno*. The steps indicated are sometimes no more than a pointing to or a counting of what is already drawn, with the much bolder line(s) provided by us in each instance identifying what is immediately being drawn or referred to. All sixty-four of these figures are drawn to the same scale.

See the note for Speech 204 (82B).

212 (82C). The words for "foot" and "feet" in Greek can be used to measure both lines and areas (that is, both *linear* and *area units*).

216 (82D). The apparent repetition here does explicitly add "feet" to the "become twice two" of Speech 214 (82D). Is Socrates hinting at the need to distinguish, and yet relate to each other, linear and area measures?

224 (82D). Mollin and Williamson ask why Socrates replaces *posoi* ("how many?"), which refers to numerable quantity, with *pêlikê tis* ("how great?" "how large?"), which refers to continuous magnitude. *An Introduction to Ancient Greek*, p. 355 n.2.

In our Appendix B diagrams we begin, in each instance of construction, as Socrates may have done, with the base of the figure immediately dealt with.

226 (82E). "Knows" translates *eidenai*. See the notes for Speeches 16 (72C) and 81 (75C).

256 (83C). At this point in their text Mollin and Williamson provide the following note: "The discussion with the slave generally takes the form of question-answer-question-answer. Here Socrates breaks the pattern, asking two questions to which the slave gives a single assenting answer. Some modern editors have seen fit to interject '*PAI. Nai.*' [Boy. Yes.] between Socrates' two questions, though there is no support for this in any of the manuscripts. May not Socrates deliberately be conflating two very different kinds of questions (one involving multiples and halves of figures and the other involving [longer and shorter] lines), thus leading the slave to apply carelessly the *habits* acquired in dealing with the one to the other?" *An Introduction to Ancient Greek*, p. 356.

Habit, which may be essential for practice, seems sometimes to get in the way of understanding, or science. See Aristotle, *Politics* 1268b23-1269a28; Thomas Aquinas, *Summa Theologica* I-II, Q. 97, A. 2, ad 1.

258 (83D). "Fine" translates *kalôs*. See the note for Speeches 113 (77B) and 404 (89C).

274 (83E-84A). "Count" translates *arithmein*, the verb derived from the word for number, *arithmos*. (According to Euclid, who is said to have been taught by pupils of Plato and who flourished about 300 BCE, numbers are restricted to what modern mathematicians call positive whole numbers.) The phrase in the text has the sense, "if you don't want to do it arithmetically". Since the square constructed on the two-foot line is too small (Speech 219 [82D]) and the square constructed on the three-foot line is too big (Speech 269 [83E]), one might try to approximate the area sought for by using fractions of units, but these could never be better than approximations. Socrates here hints that the line that would provide the eight-foot square might better be discovered by a "showing", that is, by pointing at some geometrical construction that gives up counting linear-units, but does count area-units.

Underlying this conversation between Socrates and the Boy is the great discovery of Incommensurability and the fundamental distinction between discrete (numerable) and continuous quantities. Incommensurability refers to the fact that there are definite magnitudes (lines, surfaces and solids) which do not have to one another the ratio of a number to a number. They are said to be "irrational", *alogoi*, to one another, in that their relation cannot be expressed by a ratio between numbers, or in that both cannot be measured exactly by a common measure of their own kind, although they can be distinguished and ordered in terms of the numerable areas of the squares built upon them (in modern language, in terms of "square roots"). The favorite example of Incommensurability has long been that seen in the relation of the diagonal of a square to the side of the same square. (See, e.g., Figures 58 and 64 in Appendix B of this volume.) The way Euclid puts this is to say that the diagonal and the side are incommensurable in length, but that they are "commensurable in square." That is, the area of the square constructed on the diagonal and the area of the square constructed on the side do have to one another the ratio of a (positive whole) number to a (positive whole) number. See, for the revolution in mathematical thought which allows one to speak of "irrational numbers," Jacob Klein, *Greek*

Mathematical Thought and the Origin of Algebra, Eva Brann, trans. (New York: Dover Publications, Inc., 1992). See, also, the note for Speech 82 (75C-D). See, as well, Plato, *Theaetetus* 147D sq.

Is "showing", that is, action, required for exhibiting what virtue is?

See the note for Speech 282 (84B-C).

282 (84B-C). Socrates could not have thought that his description of how the Slave-boy might once ("then") have conducted himself, or even of how he might happen to conduct himself hereafter ("now") really applied to the Boy in his circumstances. Still, what Socrates does here, in making one aware of one's ignorance, can be said to be at the heart of the philosophic enterprise. See Speech 179 (80B). See, on the teaching central to this dialogue, the note for Speeches 185-186 (80D-E). See, also, the notes for Speeches 113 (77B), 274 (83E-84A), and 404 (89C).

288 (84D). The word for "opinions", *doxa*, is connected with the term, *dokei*, which appears frequently as "it seems so" in the phrases: "Does it seem so to you?" or "It seems so to me." See, e.g., Speeches 257-258 (83D), 285-287 (84C), and 405-406 (89C).

302 (84E-85A). Is the Slave-boy recollecting, or is Socrates simply teaching him? How can one account for Meno's response in Speech 325 (85C)?

322 (85B). The Sophists were professional intellectuals who traveled among the Greek cities, expecting to be paid for exhibiting and transmitting their wisdom, *sophia*. Socrates seems to be exploiting an older use of the word *sophist*, namely, "sage", "expert". We learn, in Speeches 422-434 (91B-92D), how it is that many, if not most, Athenians used the word, its having for them something of the sense of the American expression "wise guy", if not even of the expression "con man". See, also, the notes for Speeches 2 (70B) and 426 (92A). See, as well, the note for Speech 412 (90B).

"Diagonal" translates *diametros*, literally, "the line that measures across".

The form of the phrase "Meno's boy" is the same as the form of the phrase "son of Alexidemus" in Speech 110 (76E). See the note for Speech 205 (82B).

SOCRATES AND MENO

324-325 (85B-C). See the notes for Speeches 288 (84D) and 302 (84E-85A).

334 (85D). See the note for Speech 502 (97B).

338 (85D). "Knowledge" translates *episteme*, "science", that on which (*epi*) one can hold one's place, or can stand (*steme*). How would the Boy's opinions become "knowledge"? See, on the fundamental difference between opinion and knowledge, Speeches 498-518 (97A-98B), especially Speeches 516-518 (97E-98B). See, also, the notes for Speeches 78 (75B-C) and 356 (86E-87B). See, as well, the note for Speech 82 (75C-D).

348 (86A). See Plato, *Republic* 614A-621; Plato, *Phaedo* 105E-115A.

355 (86C-D). Compare the question put by Meno at the beginning of this dialogue.

356 (86D). Bluck notes, "True freedom, of course, presupposes self-mastery." *Plato's Meno*, p. 321. See the note for Speech 26 (73A).

356 (86E). "Hypothetically" translates *ex hypotheseôs*; "hypothesis", "something put" or "a putting" (*thesis*), "under" (*hypo*), for a support or a foundation, a "supposition" (*sub-positio*), a "hypothesis".

This method is contrasted with dialectic in Plato's *Republic*. In *Republic* 511 this habit or condition of the mathematicians is spoken of as not being "rational intelligence", or "intellect" (*nous*), as is dialectic, but rather "thinking" (*dianoia*), something in between opinion and rational intelligence. See, also, Jacob Klein, *A Commentary on Plato's Meno*, pp. 120-125 and our note for Speech 82 (75C-D).

The word translated here as "figure" (*chôrion*) is that used during the Slave-boy demonstration where we translate it as "area". "Figure" is the more technical translation. See the note for Speech 204 (82B).

356 (86E-87B). There have been dozens of suggestions published about what geometrical problem is being referred to in this passage. A survey of various interpretations may be found in Bluck, *Plato's Meno* pp. 441-61. See, also, Thomas L. Heath, *A Manual of Greek Mathematics* (New York: Dover Publications, 1963), pp. 178-80; Wilbur Richard Knorr, *The Ancient Tradition of Geometric Problems* (New York: Dover Publications, 1986), pp. 71-74, 92-94; John E. Thomas, *Musings on the Meno* (The Hague: Martinus Nijhoff Publishing, 1980), pp. 165-70; the note for Speech 357 (87C).

One generally (but not universally) accepted conjecture (developed by S.H. Butcher in 1888) uses this kind of illustration:

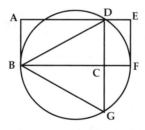

"The problem seems to be that of inscribing in a circle a triangle (BDG) equal in area to a given rectangle (ABCD)." W.R.M. Lamb, ed., Plato *Meno* (Loeb Classical Library Edition), p. 325, n. 6. See, also, E. Seymer Thompson, *The Meno ofPlato* (Cambridge: W. Heffer & Sons, 1961), pp. 148f; Richard S. Bluck, *Plato's Meno* (Cambridge: Harvard University Press, 1961), pp. 442-44.

The following relations might usefully be noticed among elements of this illustration: BDG is a "triangular figure" "inscribed in this circle." BDG is equal in area to the rectangular figure ABCD. ABCD is "appli[ed]" to part

(BC) of the diameter of the circle, BF ("the given line of itself"), "fall[ing] short" by the figure CDEF which is based on the remaining part (CF) of the diameter BF. If BC:CD::CD:CF, figure CDEF is similar to ("like") figure ABCD. If this is indeed so, then one result somehow follows; if not, there is another result.

What more needs to be either conjectured or noticed here? How, if at all, does Socrates' difficult and obscure problem illuminate the difficulties and obscurities found in any inquiry as to how virtue is acquired, used, and transmitted?

Jacob Klein connects the geometric problem used here to the discussion of virtue in this way: "[T]he analogy to be drawn is as follows: the given space is (or is not) 'inscribable' into the given circle, *if* the area which is equal to the given space has (or has not) the relation of 'similarity' to another area; excellence [virtue] is (or is not) 'teachable'—inscribable into the soul, as it were—*if* it has (or has not) the relation of 'similarity' or 'likeness' to something else in the soul. What is this 'something else'? It is playfully treated by Socrates as an unknown 'fourth proportional' in his next sentence.... The interrogative twist [87b5]... underscores that what is being considered 'from a supposition' is the 'likeness', not identity, of *aretê* ["virtue"] and *epistêmê* ["knowledge"]. *A Commentary on Plato's Meno,* pp. 208-09. See, also, the notes for Speeches 78 (75B-C) and 338 (85D). Is knowledge the unknown "fourth proportional" referred to here?

356 (87C). Consider the final sentence of this speech in the light of Speech 348 (86A).

357 (87C). It should be noticed that Meno, who had *not* been reluctant to challenge various suggestions made by Socrates, does not register any protest about the geometrical problem that has just been used. Had Meno been helped by drawings provided by Socrates? See the note for Speech 66 (74E).

364 (87D). Mollin and Williamson note that this phrase, "virtue is a good thing in itself", might also mean, "it [is] a good thing, [namely] virtue", or "[it] is [the] good itself". *An Introduction to Ancient Greek*, p. 371, n.3.

366 (87D). For the first alternative, consider Speech 548 (99A) to the end of the dialogue; for the second alternative, consider Speeches 380-388 (88A-D).

374 (87E). Compare Speeches 148-166 (78C-79A).

382 (88B). "Prudence" translates *phronêsis*, the virtue of practical thoughtfulness, good practical judgment, practical intelligence, practical wisdom. ("Prudence" comes from the Latin *prudens*, short for *providens*, "looking ahead".) In some contexts, especially ethical and political contexts, "prudence" seems to be indistinguishable from *sophia* (which, in this translation, is rendered as "wisdom")—more in the sense of theoretical wisdom. See the notes for Speeches 2 (70B) and 26 (73A).

384 (88B). Editors differ as to whether the participles "learned" and "trained for" apply to "moderation" and "readiness to learn", or stand by themselves. In accordance with the latter interpretation, the clause after the semicolon can be translated as, "when *things* are learned" instead of "when *they* are learned". See Bluck, *Plato's Meno*, pp. 332-33.

386 (88C). "Happiness" translates *eudaimonia*, which means literally "the state of having in one (or being in) a good spirit". Our old-fashioned, somewhat theological, word "felicity" comes close to it. Consider Aristotle, *Nicomachean Ethics* 1144a7-8, 1144b1-32. Consider, also, the note for Speech 136 (78A).

388 (88D). Notice the shifts in Speeches 382-388 (88B-D) from "knowledge" to "intelligence" to "prudence". See, on prudence, the notes for Speeches 26 (73A) and 384 (88B).

392 (88E). "Mistakenly" translates *hêmartêmenôs*. The word *hamartia*, connected with the same verb, means "mistake" or "error". It has also been interpreted, in connection with Aristotle's *Poetics* (e.g., 1453a10), as "tragic flaw", an error of character. It is the word in the Greek Bible which is regularly translated as "sin". See Laurence Berns, "Aristotle's *Poetics*," in Joseph Cropsey, ed., *Ancients and Moderns* (New York: Basic Books, 1964), e.g., pp. 77-79.

396 (89A). E. Seymer Thompson puts the argument in Speeches 388-396 (88C-89A) "in bare syllogistic form":

> All *the beneficial* is *prudence.*
> All *virtue* is *beneficial.*
> [Therefore] All *virtue* is *prudence.*

The Meno of Plato (Cambridge: W. Heffer & Sons, 1961), p. 161 (the italicized words in this syllogism are provided in Greek by Thompson). This Thompson edition of the *Meno* (originally published by Macmillan in 1901) includes two hundred pages of detailed commentary on the text of the dialogue. See the note for Speech 490 (96E).

396-399 (89A). However, do not some human beings appear to be naturally prudent? Consider the provisions in Plato's *Republic* for identifying and rearing appropriately the children naturally fitted for virtue. See, e.g., 374E-376C, 485A-487A.

400 (89B). "On the Acropolis" translates *en akropolei*. The Acropolis is the *akros*, "the highest point", of the *polis*, "the city". It is likely to be the best-guarded part of the city, the citadel. In Athens public treasures were safeguarded in temples on the Acropolis. Seals were used to designate public property. Compare 456 (94B) and its note.

402 (89B-C). Is the denial of the hypothetical argument of Speech 400 (89B) sufficient to establish this conclusion?

404 (89C). "Rightly", in this and the next few speeches, translates *kalôs*, the adverbial form of the word for "beautiful" and "handsome". See the notes for Speeches 113 (77B) and 494 (97A).

The word *kalôs* has a broad range of meanings—from the moral beauty of the noble or honorable, through the deftness of the skillful, to the intellectual beauty, as here, of a nice, fine or elegant argument or proof. "[O]ften it implies that some simplification (warranted or not) has been made. *Kalôs* is a signal that a difficulty has been got around, and that the way of the argument has now been made easier." Seth Benardete, "The Right, the True and the Beautiful," *Glotta* 41, nos. 1-2 (1963): 55-56. The word's opposite, *aisxros* or *aisxos*, ranges from "ugly" to "base", "shameful", and "disgraceful". See the notes for Speeches 113 (73B) and 494 (97A). See, also, the note for Speech 113 (77B).

406 (89C). The words heretofore translated by us as "right" and "rightly" [*orthos*], especially in Speeches 378 (88A), 390 (88E), and 392 (88E), adhere more closely here to the notion of "correctness". See the notes for Speeches 494 (97A) and 502 (97B). "Soundness" here translates *hugiês*, in Speech 112 (89C) it is translated as "health".

412 (90A). "The reference [to Ismenias and Polycrates] is uncertain; it may be to the bribing of the Theban Ismenias by the wealthy Polycrates to aid [Anytus and the other exiled Athenian democrats] in restoring [in 403 BCE] the Athenian democracy during the oligarchic rule of the 'Thirty Tyrants'." Mollin and Williamson, *An Introduction to Ancient Greek*, p. 377 n.7. Compare Plato, *Meno* (Loeb Classical Library Edition), pp. 334-45, nn. 1, 2. See the note for Speech 412 (90B).

SOCRATES AND ANYTUS

412 (90B). Anytus was a leader of the democratic party in Athens. He eventually became one of the three accusers of Socrates. See Plato, *Apology of Socrates*. Meno's social connections elsewhere seem to have been more aristocratic than they seem to be in Athens, where he evidently enjoyed the status of a guest-friend of Anytus. See the note for Speech 116 (77C).

We are introduced in this speech to the theme, shortly to be developed, of fathers educating sons. We never hear, in this dialogue, how well Anytus did as a father, nor about how well Socrates educated his three sons. It has been said that none of their children ever distinguished themselves. See, on father-and-son relations, the note for Speech 429 (92B). See also Speech 460 (95A).

See, on Anytus' presence at this gathering, the note for Speech 552 (99B).

A somewhat sympathetic account of Anytus' career is provided in the following entry taken from *The Oxford Classical Dictionary*, p. 65:

> *Anytus* (5th-4th c. B.C.), a wealthy Athenian and a democratic leader. General in 409 B.C., he failed to prevent the loss of Pylus, and is said to have escaped condemnation only by bribery. After the [Peloponessian

War], he was one of the restorers of democracy with Thrasybulus, proving himself an honest and moderate politician. Plato (*Meno* 90f.) introduces him as a well-bred man, but a passionate enemy of the Sophists. He probably did not belong to the circle of Socrates, as some sources hint. He became Socrates' chief accuser, less for private reasons than from an honest belief that he was doing the best for Athens. Accounts about his banishment and murder may be later inventions.

The reader is challenged to assess this perhaps standard scholarly appraisal in the light of the Anytus exhibited in Plato's *Meno*. See the note for Speech 153 (78C). *The Oxford Classical Dictionary* has no separate entry on our Meno.

See, on Plato's *Apology of Socrates*, George Anastaplo, *Human Being and Citizen: Essays on Virtue, Freedom and the Common Good* (Chicago: Swallow Press, 1975), pp. 8f, 203f.

420 (90E). Some editors reject the phrase "seek to learn from those… the student". We retain it, preferring to try to make sense of the manuscript, rather than adding language in brackets which is said by some scholars to be implied by the manuscript. See, e.g., Bluck, *Plato's Meno*, p. 351.

422 (91A). Some translations understand "guest-friend of ours" as "guest-friend of yours". The Greek is not unambiguous.

"People" translates *anthrôpoi*, which (in the singular) is translated elsewhere as "human being" or "man". "Man" translates words from the root *andr-*, from which are derived the words for "courage", *andreia*, for "image of a man", or "statue", *andrias*, and for "sculptor", *andriantopoios* ("maker of statues"). *Andros* suggests the "manly man", or the "he-man".

"Manage" translates *dioikein*. See the note for Speech 24 (73B).

422 (91A-B). The words "in order to learn" here are a well-considered scholarly conjecture, perhaps anticipating "wants to learn" further on in this Speech. See Bluck, *Plato's Meno*, pp. 181, 353.

424 (91B). See, on the Sophists, the note for Speech 322 (85B).

425 (91C). Heracles' career included a period of madness during which he slaughtered his own wife and children. See, for example, Euripides, *Heracles Furens*. See, also, the note for Speech 429 (92B).

Xenos, translated here as "foreigner", is translated elsewhere as "guest-friend" (a special relationship of hospitality between families from different cities) and as "stranger". Consider our word "xenophobia". See, also, Speeches 156 (78D), 422 (91A), and 426-427 (91C-92D), and the note for Speech 156 (78D).

A participial form of "corruption" is used in the official charge against Socrates in 399 BCE. See Plato, *Apology of Socrates* 24B. See, also, Xenophon,

Memorabilia [of Socrates], I, i; Diogenes Laertius, *Lives of Eminent Philosophers*, II, 40. See, as well, the notes for Speeches 412 (90B) and 426 (92A).

426 (91D). Protagoras, of Abdera in Thrace (c. 485-c. 415 BCE), is a major character in the Platonic dialogue named after him. See the notes for Speeches 426 (92A) and 469 (95C).

Protagorean relativism is extensively described, analyzed and refuted in Plato's *Theaetetus* 151D-183C. Socrates quotes him as saying, "Man [the human being] is the measure of all things, of the things which are, that they are, and of the things which are not, that they are not." *Theaetetus* 152A. By making "man" the center (in contrast to "nature" or "God"), Protagoras has been said to anticipate the founding of modern philosophy. Socrates' critique of the epistemology, physics, and ontology of Protagorean relativism has thereby been taken to be a critique of modern, as well as of ancient, man-centered relativism. See the note for Speech 194 (81E). See, also, the note for Speech 82 (75C-D).

Phidias, of Athens (c. 490-c. 417 BCE), was said by ancient writers to be the greatest of the mortal sculptors of Greece. He was important in the adornment of the Athenian Acropolis during Pericles' administration. Some of his work is said to survive in the metopes, frieze, and pediment of the Parthenon, which he designed, supervised, and in some parts sculpted. See the note for Speech 514 (97D).

426 (91E). See, for Protagoras' policy on charging and collecting fees, Plato, *Protagoras* 328B-C. See, also, Plato, *Theaetetus* 161B sq.

426 (92A). From Anytus' point of view, what Socrates asks here about Protagoras— whether he, having lived nearly seventy years, had artfully corrupted his associates for forty years—applies to Socrates himself. The fact that Socrates never demanded pay for what he did seems not to have been important for Anytus, judging from his prominent role as an accuser at Socrates' trial. Socrates, from Anytus' perspective, is just another kind of Sophist. See, for Socrates' way of distinguishing his life in philosophy from sophistry, Plato, *Apology of Socrates*; Xenophon, *Apology of Socrates*; Xenophon, *Memorabilia [of Socrates]*. See, on the distinction between knowingly corrupting and unwittingly corrupting the youth touched upon in the penultimate sentence of this speech, Plato, *Apology of Socrates* 25C-26A.

However this may be, one might expect Socrates to argue that the salutary effect of those who receive pay for their services is to be inferred only if those who pay understand both what they are paying for and that it is good for them. The argument here may be meant ironically, to appeal to a man whose father made his money by himself. See Speech 412 (90A). See, on Plato's *Apology*, the note for Speech 412 (90B).

427 (92B). See Speeches 179 (80B) and 459 (94E-95A).

429 (92B). Anytus, after having been moved to invoke Heracles in Speech 425 (91C), returns to invoking Zeus, the father of Heracles. See Speech 421

(90E). See, on Heracles, the note for Speech 425 (91C). See, also, the notes for Speeches 412 (90A) and 412 (90B).

434 (92C). "Diviner" translates *mantis*, which has often been rendered as "prophet", but not in this translation. See Speech 558 (99D). *Mantis* is related to the Greek word *mania*. Our English word "prophet" is derived from the Greek word, *prophêtês*, which means "properly one who speaks for a god and interprets his will to man." Liddell and Scott, *Greek-English Lexicon*. The word *prophêtês* does not appear in this dialogue. Nor is there any explicit reference to philosophy or philosophers. In Plato's *Timaeus*, the *mantis*, "one who utters oracles" while not in his right mind but in a state of divine frenzy, is distinguished by Timaeus from the *prophêtês* who, in his right mind, judges and interprets such oracles. *Timaeus* 71A-72C, especially 71E-72C. See the note for Speech 558 (99D). But see also Plato's *Phaedrus* 244A-245C.

434 (92D). The other reference to a "hereditary", or special family, relationship occurs in Speech 156 (78D). See the note for Speech 116 (77C).

437 (92E). "Gentleman" translates the appellation *kalôs kagothôs*, literally, "a noble and good man".

Compare Speech 2 (71A). Compare, also, Speech 469 (95C).

440 (93C). Themistocles (c. 528-c. 462 BCE) was the successful leader of Athens during the Persian War. He ended his life exiled from Athens. See *The Oxford Classical Dictionary*, p. 892.

444 (93D). "Upright" translates *orthos*. The Greek root *orth-* is at the bottom of a large family of meanings, from morals to mathematics, just as the Latin root *rect-* is in the corresponding English words "right", "correct", "rectitude", and "rectangle". (It may be seen as well in the German word *Recht*.) See the notes for Speeches 406 (89C), 494 (97A), and 562 (99E). See, also, the note for Speech 502 (97B).

Sophos is translated here as "skilled". In Speeches 448 (93E) and 450 (93E), *sophos* is translated as "wise".

448 (93E). See the note for Speech 444 (93D). See, also, the note for Speech 440 (93C).

452 (94A). Herodotus called the man known as "Aristides the Just" (c. 520-c. 468 BCE) "the best and most just man in Athens". He was once ostracized by the Athenians. See, for his relations with Themistocles, Herodotus, *History*, 8. 78-83.

454 (94A). See, on Lysimachus, the note for Speech 456 (94B).

454 (94B). Pericles (c. 495-429 BCE) was the leader of Athens at the beginning of the ill-fated Peloponnesian War. See Thucydides, *History of the Peloponnesian War*, II, xii-lxv. Pericles is discussed in Plato's *Protagoras*, *Menexenus*, *Phaedrus*, *Gorgias*, and *Symposium*.

See, on Paralus and Xanthippus, the note for Speech 456 (94B).

456 (94B). Pericles' very talented, mercurial ward Alcibiades, to whom Socrates was once close, is not mentioned. See Plato's *Symposium*; *The Oxford Classical Dictionary*, p. 31. See, also, Xenophon, *Memorabilia [of Socrates]*, I, ii, 12-28, 39-47. See, as well, Speech 400 (89B).

Lysimachus, son of Aristides (Speech 454 [94A]), and Melesias, son of Thucydides (Speech 456 [94C]), appear in Plato's *Laches* consulting with Socrates about how to bring up *their* sons. Does such a concern on the part of Lysimachus and Melesias suggest that they turned out somewhat better than is indicated by Socrates in talking to Anytus? Lysimachus complains that their fathers (Aristides and Thucydides) had neglected their sons because they were so busy with public affairs. See Plato *Laches* 179A.

Paralus and Xanthippus, sons of Pericles (Speech 454 [94B]), appear in Plato's *Protagoras* (315A) as part of the amusing train of listeners to Protagoras. See, also, *Protagoras* 319D-320A, where Socrates again speaks of Pericles' failure to pass his own virtues on to his sons.

456 (94C). This Thucydides (flourished 449 BCE) is not the historian, but rather an aristocratic political rival of Pericles. He, too, was once ostracized by the Athenians. See *The Oxford Classical Dictionary*, p. 902.

We have here pairs of political rivals from two generations: Themistocles and Aristides, Pericles and Thucydides. The first and third were more populist democrats, the second and fourth more conservative aristocrats. See Bluck, *Plato's Meno*, p. 369 n. 47; Mollin and Williamson, *An Introduction to Ancient Greek*, p. 391.

459 (94E-95A). Anytus supposes, correctly, that Socrates is not a political innocent: he has lived almost seventy years in Athens, has continually spoken at length with all sorts of citizens (and non-citizens), and has just exhibited a keen interest in and knowledge of Athenian political gossip.

Socrates' discussion here favors neither of the dominant politically-partisan groupings of Athens, but raises questions instead, as Anytus understands him, about the political class as a whole. Anytus, quite naturally, seems to take the argument personally. See Diogenes Laertius, *Lives of Eminent Philosophers*, II, 38. See, also, Speech 179 (80B).

SOCRATES AND MENO

467 (95C). See, for example, Plato *Gorgias* 455D sq.

469 (95C). "Most people" (*oi polloi*) is, literally, "the many".

Leo Strauss spoke of this as the "in a way, most surprising moment in the dialogue." Strauss, "Plato's Political Philosophy: The *Meno*," Lecture 11, p. 7. Meno is not simply a follower of Gorgias, who himself laughs at Sophists like Protagoras insofar as they claim to be able to teach virtue. Meno himself seems to be torn between the opinion that the Sophists can teach virtue and the opinion that they cannot. Meno is not much concerned with the fundamental question (What is virtue?), but is very much concerned instead with the question of how to acquire it, perhaps only in order to display himself engaging in "policy" debates back home about the training and supervision of citizens. If Protagoras is right, and Meno has not taken the kind of virtue-course that Protagoras offered, then Meno's own virtue is deficient. This, Strauss suggested, explains why Meno approaches Socrates with his abrupt opening question: he hopes that Socrates might prove to be an arbiter between Gorgian sophistry and Protagorean sophistry. See Plato's *Gorgias* and *Protagoras*. See, on Meno as acquisitive, the notes for Speeches 1 (70A), 113 (77B) and 526 (98D).

470 (95C-E). Theognis of Megara flourished about 520 BCE. See, for text and sources, Bluck, *Plato's Meno*, pp. 392-94.

474 (95E-96A). *Is* there a contradiction (that is, "opposite things" said)? Or is the poet talking about different natural endowments? Why does Meno not raise such questions? See, for the uses of "nature" (*phusis*) and "natural" in the dialogue, Speeches 1 (70A), 398-402 (89A-B), and 526-30 (98C-D). See, also, the notes for Speeches 2 (71B) and 82 (75C-D).

476 (96A-B). "Acknowledged" translates the passive form of the verb *homologein* (literally, "to say or to think the same"). This, in the perfect active form, is translated "have agreed". See Speeches 482 (96C) and 483 (96C). The same implicit passive form is also translated "recognized as" or "regarded as".

480 (96C). Granting that everything teachable is learnable (see Speech 408 [89D]), is everything learnable teachable? How do the first teachers become such?

484 (96C). "There appear to be" can also be translated "there are manifestly". Socrates does not supply the word that would make it one or the other. One argument for "manifestly" could be that Socrates is here introducing the minor premise of a syllogism.

490 (96D). See Speech 82 (75E) and its note. Socrates, just after concluding that virtue could not be teachable, seems to blame Meno's and his own teachers for not having adequately taught virtue to Meno and Socrates.

490 (96E). Thompson notes that "the state of the discussion as it stands now is represented by two hypothetical syllogisms, as follows:

> 1. If virtue is knowledge, it is teachable:
> But virtue is knowledge:
> Therefore virtue is teachable.
>
> 2. If virtue is knowledge, it is teachable:
> But virtue is not teachable:
> Therefore virtue is not knowledge.

The minor premise of each of these two syllogisms contradicts the conclusion of the other." *The Meno of Plato*, p. 214. As for the shared major premise, see

Speech 356 (86D-E, 87B). Can the premises here be modified so as to arrive at non-contradictory conclusions?

494 (97A). "Rightly" translates *orthôs* and "right" translates *kalôs*. All the other instances of "right" or "rightly" in this section of the dialogue refer to *orthôs*, the adverb for "correct", "right", "straight". Consider our cognate "orthodox", which in Greek would mean "right" or "correct opinion". See the notes for Speeches 406 (89C) and 502 (97B).

498 (97A). See, on Larissa, the note for Speech 1 (70B).

502 (97B). Socrates does not seem to distinguish here (or in Speech 504 [97B]) "right" (*orthê*) "opinion" (*doxa*) from "true" (*alêthês*) "opinion" (*doxa*). Is this because Socrates is ignoring here the distinction between theory and practice? Or is it that the distinction between all opinion, on the one hand, and knowledge, on the other hand (Speeches 330-334 [85C-D] and 512-518 [97D-98B]), renders the distinction between theory and practice meaningless among opinions? (*Alethes* means, literally, "unhidden".) See, also, the note for Speech 518 (98B). See, for the development elsewhere of the distinction between theory and practice, Plato, *Republic* 472E-473A. See, as well, the notes for Speeches 434 (92C) and 520-522 (98B-C).

See, on *orthos*, the notes for Speeches 406 (89C), 444 (93D), 494 (97A), and 562 (99E).

512 (97D). See, on Daedalus, Plato, *Euthyphro* 11B sq (where Daedalus is identified as an ancestor of Socrates). See, also, the note for Speech 514 (97D).

514 (97D). "[A]mong the marvels attributed to this legendary craftsman [Daedalus] was the making of statues which moved—perhaps a mythical representation of the development of sculpture to suggest the human body in motion rather than [in] repose." Mollin and Williamson, *An Introduction to Ancient Greek*, p. 401. See the note for Speech 426 (91D).

516 (97E-98A). Socrates, both before and after this speech, seems to use "right opinion" and "true opinion" interchangeably. Here (and in Speech 526 [98C-D]), he uses both terms in the same speech. See the note for Speech 406 (89C).

516 (98A). "Causes" translates *aitias*. This word and its adjectival form are also common legal terms for "charge", "accusation", "guilt", "credit". The basic notion seems to be that it is what is responsible for something, so that it can sometimes mean a reason for something. Consider Speech 2 (70B) ("the one responsible…is Gorgias"). Consider, also, our word *aetiology*.

To "bind" right opinions "means to find reasons for them in one's own thinking." Klein, *A Commentary on the Meno*, p. 248.

518 (98B). Is Socrates, in making "images and conjectures", like Daedalus? Consider Speech 356 (86D-88C).

Speeches 516 (97E-98A) and 518 (98B) not only distinguish opinion from knowledge but also indicate how one moves through and from opinions to knowledge by binding them "with causes by reasoning." Despite the essential defect of opinions, not all opinions are equal. True opinions are better than false opinions. Are we not supplied with a standard for distinguishing among true opinions? The more a true opinion is supported by evidence of causes through reasoning, the better it is.

See the note for Speech 502 (97D). See, also, the note for Speech 434 (92C).

520-522 (98B-C). Consider similar discussions by Aristotle. Knowledge and art, he says, arise for human beings out of experience. See Aristotle, *Metaphysics* 980b28-981a13. Art is defined as a steady capacity to make in accordance with a true and rational account. See Aristotle *Nicomachean Ethics* 1140a9-11. "As concerns acting, experience does not seem to differ from art at all, but those people with experience are even more successful than those who have a rational account but are without experience (and this is because experience is awareness of particulars, but art is awareness of universals, and all actions and becomings are concerned with the particular...)." *Metaphysics* 981a13-17. Aristotle agrees with Socrates that opinion is properly of that which is variable and that particulars are indeed variable.

526 (98D). "Nor are they acquired" is in most manuscripts. "Some commentators think better sense is made if *out[e]* [the Greek for "nor"] is considered a scribe's miscopying of *ont[a]* [the Greek for "they are"]." Mollin and Williamson, *An Introduction to Ancient Greek*, p. 403. Thus, the latter part of this speech could be translated, "and neither of these two is natural to human beings—neither knowledge nor true opinion, but is acquired—or does it seem to you that neither of them is by nature?" Consider the opening speech of this dialogue. Consider, also, the note for Speech 113 (77B). Consider, as well, the note for Speech 2 (71B).

548 (99A). Our translation follows the reading of the manuscripts (*epigignetai*, "consequent to"). In defending the conjecture followed here by most modern editors, Thompson argues, "But Virtue has never been described as an *epigennêma* ("consequence") of Knowledge." *The Meno of Plato*, p. 253. But has not this possibility been indicated in the very speech by Socrates that precedes this one, and in other places? Virtue (that is, virtuous action and character) seems to be said in these passages to be consequent upon direction from true opinion or knowledge. See the note for Speech 338 (85D).

552 (99B). Anytus, then, would still seem to be present at this discussion or at least visible to Socrates and Meno. The word "here" could be thought of as accompanied by some gesture. See, also, Speeches 561 (99E) and 564 (100B). Klein speaks of Anytus as being present, "phantom-like." *A Commentary on Plato's Meno*, p. 253. It might be wondered as well whether Anytus had joined this gathering before he is referred to in Speech 412 (96A).

The lines drawn by Socrates for the Slave-boy, even if routinely erased as they proceed, can all be considered to linger "phantom-like" (and, as such, are all incorporated in Figure 64 of Appendix B of this volume). See the notes for Speeches 204 (82B) and 206 (82C).

554 (99B). "Good judgment based on opinion" translates *eudoxia*, which also means "good reputation".

558 (99D). "Divinely inspired" translates *enthousiazein*: *thous* is a contracted form of *theos*, "god"; *enthous* is, then, "having a god within". The English words "enthused", "enthusiasm", and "enthusiastic" are derived from this root. See the note for Speech 434 (92C).

560 (99D). Laconians is another name for the Spartans (or Lacedemonians). Laconia is the region which contains Sparta.

561 (99E). See Speech 552 (99B). See, also, Bluck, *Plato's Meno*, pp. 432-33.

562 (99E). "Rightly" here is not *orthôs*, which is more in the sense of "correctly", but rather *kalôs*, which is more in the sense of "nobly". See the notes for Speeches 113 (77B) and 404 (89C).

562 (100A). Homer's lines are from his *Odyssey*, X, 494-495, where it is said that this power was bestowed on Tiresias by the goddess Persephone. See, on Persephone, the notes for Speeches 110 (76E) and 194 (81B-C). Tiresias, who figures prominently in the stories of Oedipus and Antigone, is associated with Thebes. See, on Thebes, the note for Speech 412 (90A).

"Shadows" are critical in the Cave of Plato's *Republic*, Book VII.

564 (100B-C). Jacob Klein, as he prepares to conclude his study of the *Meno* by reviewing Socrates' account of "the result of the entire dialogue" (in Speeches 562-564 [99E-100C]), observes, "Let us not forget: he is talking to Meno." *A Commentary on Plato's Meno*, p. 255.

See the notes for Speeches 274 (83E-84A) and 282 (84B-C).

APPENDIX A
OATHS IN THE *MENO*

I. The oaths are collected here for each of the characters who utter them:

Socrates   1. "by the gods" (Speech 10 [71D])
              2. "by Zeus" (Speech 404 [89C])

Meno   1. "by Zeus" (Speech 197 [82A])
              2. "by Zeus" (Speech 463 [95B])
              3. "By Zeus" (Speech 477 [96B])
              4. "By Zeus" (Speech 517 [98A])

Slave-boy 1. "by Zeus" (Speech 245 [83B])
              2. "by Zeus" (Speech 275 [84A])

Anytus   1. "by Zeus" (Speech 421 [90E])
              2. "by Heracles" (Speech 425 [91C])
              3. "by Zeus" (Speech 429 [92B])
              4. "by Zeus" (Speech 451 [93E])

II. The oaths are collected here in the order in which they were uttered:

1.	Socrates:	"by the gods"	(Speech 10 [71D])
2.	Meno:	"by Zeus"	(Speech 197 [82A])
3.	Slave-boy:	"by Zeus"	(Speech 245 [83B])
4.	Slave-boy:	"by Zeus"	(Speech 275 [84A])
5.	Socrates:	"by Zeus"	(Speech 404 [89C])
6.	Anytus:	"by Zeus"	(Speech 421 [90E])
7.	Anytus:	"by Heracles"	(Speech 425 [91C])
8.	Anytus:	"by Zeus"	(Speech 429 [92B])
9.	Anytus:	"by Zeus"	(Speech 451 [93E])
10.	Meno:	"by Zeus"	(Speech 463 [95B])
11.	Meno:	"By Zeus"	(Speech 477 [96B])
12.	Meno:	"By Zeus"	(Speech 517 [98A])

APPENDIX B
GEOMETRICAL DIAGRAMS

These figures track the steps in the geometrical developments from Speech 204 (82B) through Speech 322 (85B) of the *Meno*. The steps suggested here are sometimes no more than a pointing to or a counting of what is already there, with the bolder line(s) in each instance identifying what is immediately being drawn, referred to, or counted. All sixty-four figures are drawn to the same scale. See the notes for Speeches 204 (82B) and 206 (82C). See, also, the notes for Speeches 224 (82D) and 552 (99B).

Fourteen of the figures are repeated in this fashion:

I.	3, 6	VIII.	29, 35, 39
II.	8, 10	IX.	34, 37
III.	17, 22, 24, 26	X.	48, 52
IV.	18, 21, 23, 25, 27, 30	XI.	49, 53
V.	19, 40, 46	XII.	50, 55, 59
VI.	20, 45	XIII.	51, 62
VII.	28, 31	XIV.	58, 63

FIGURE 1 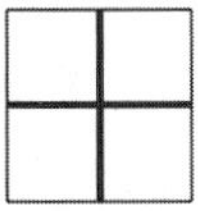   FIGURE 2 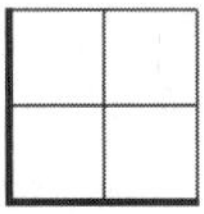   FIGURE 3    FIGURE 4 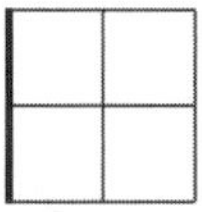   FIGURE 5

FIGURE 6 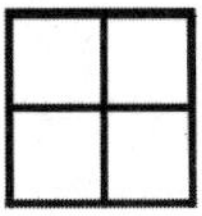   FIGURE 7 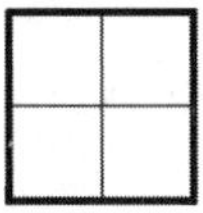   FIGURE 8    FIGURE 9 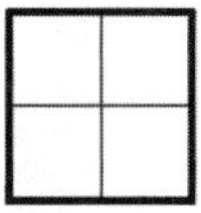   FIGURE 10

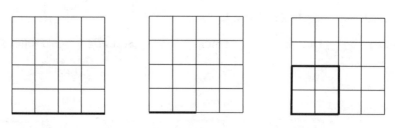

FIGURE 11   FIGURE 12   FIGURE 13

FIGURE 14   FIGURE 15   FIGURE 16

FIGURE 17   FIGURE 18   FIGURE 19

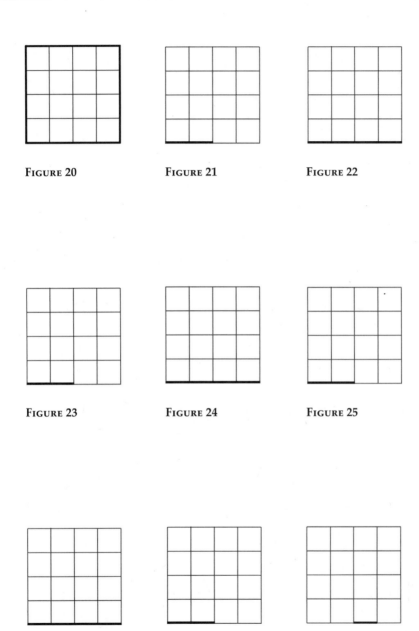

FIGURE 20   FIGURE 21   FIGURE 22

FIGURE 23   FIGURE 24   FIGURE 25

FIGURE 26   FIGURE 27   FIGURE 28

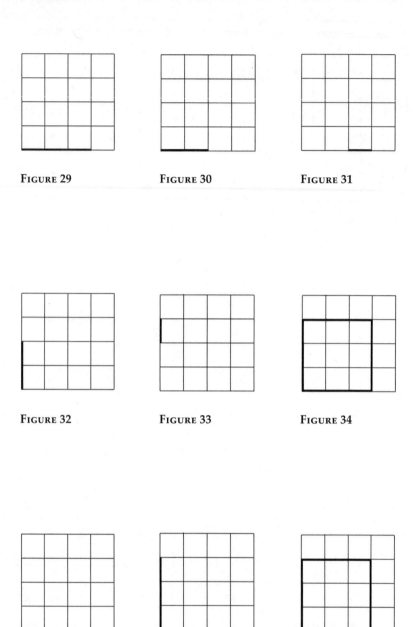

FIGURE 29   FIGURE 30   FIGURE 31

FIGURE 32   FIGURE 33   FIGURE 34

FIGURE 35   FIGURE 36   FIGURE 37

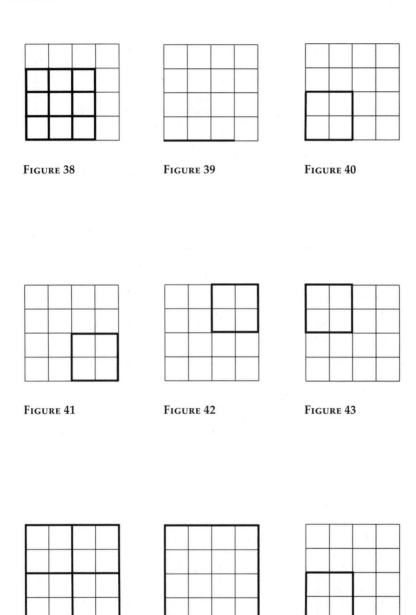

FIGURE 38

FIGURE 39

FIGURE 40

FIGURE 41

FIGURE 42

FIGURE 43

FIGURE 44

FIGURE 45

FIGURE 46

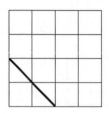

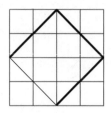

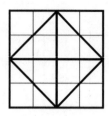

FIGURE 47   FIGURE 48   FIGURE 49

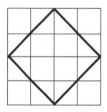

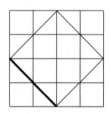

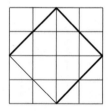

FIGURE 50   FIGURE 51   FIGURE 52

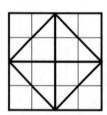

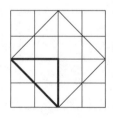

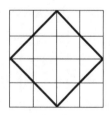

FIGURE 53   FIGURE 54   FIGURE 55

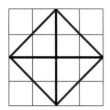

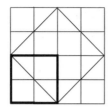

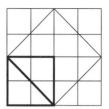

FIGURE 56   FIGURE 57   FIGURE 58

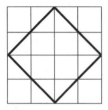

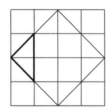

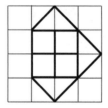

FIGURE 59   FIGURE 60   FIGURE 61

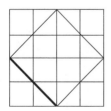

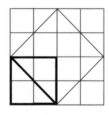

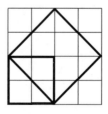

FIGURE 62   FIGURE 63   FIGURE 64